DAVID LEE teaches at Hagerstown Junior College in Maryland. He has taught fly fishing to beginners of all ages. Several of his articles on fly fishing have been published in leading magazines, and he has made a series of television programs on fly fishing for the West Virginia Department of Natural Resources. During the fishing season, he conducts a guide service for fly fishers.

David Lee

FLY FISHING
A BEGINNER'S GUIDE

With ILLUSTRATIONS BY
Daniel D. Feaser

PHOTOGRAPHS BY
Katherine G. Lee

FOREWORD BY
John Randolph
Managing Editor, *Fly Fisherman Magazine*

Prentice Hall Press • New York

Library of Congress Cataloging-in-Publication Data
Lee, David, 1942–
  Fly fishing.

  Includes bibliographies and index.
  1. Fly fishing. I. Title
SH456.L43   799.1'2   81-12110
                 AACR2

ISBN 0-13-322529-1 (pbk.)

Published in 1986 by Prentice Hall Press
A Division of Simon & Schuster, Inc.
Gulf + Western Building
One Gulf + Western Plaza
New York, NY 10023

Originally published by Prentice-Hall, Inc.
PRENTICE HALL PRESS is a trademark of Simon & Schuster, Inc.

Manufactured in the United States of America

10 9 8 7 6 5 4 3 2

for Katherine

CONTENTS

x

Contents

FOREWORD

By John Randolph
Managing Editor,
Fly Fisherman Magazine

The Mettawee River looked promising. Although the water was riseless, it was colored and the fish could not see clearly and would hit foolishly. Clouds hung blackly over the valley but separated now and then to let in long shafts of gold October sunlight. A herd of cows lay crouched at streamside below a barnyard. The weather, the cows, and the season all seemed to be between things.

Jamie Woods had reached the stream before us. When we pulled off the road and parked, he quit fishing and came downstream, pausing for a second behind a bush.

"They're taking grasshoppers," he said. "Three trout."

Jamie helped my son, John, rig a grasshopper pattern, and then we moved upstream to the first good lie. He showed John the way to fish a hopper, casting out to the bank and letting the fly drift without drag down a nice glide. A trout rose to the hopper and missed.

"See him?" Jamie asked.

John cast to the fish, but the fly dragged.

"You can't let it drag," I said. "Trout won't abide drag. They get suspicious the way a wild turkey becomes alarmed by movement. Free drift is what you need to fool trout."

John fished and his backcast caught in thistles and grass. The fly line got all wound around things, and when he cast a wind blew downriver and filled his line with wind knots. He became exasperated the way I do when I have big plans and the line tangles. Jamie moved upstream and then motioned for us to come to where he stood.

"He can fish here a little easier. He won't catch his backcast so much and there are fish rising in the pool," Jamie called.

The sun broke through the clouds for a minute and lighted a yellow elm beside an old iron bridge on the Mettawee. There were trout rising below the bridge in the clear, dark pool and the cows lay upstream, on fall-green grass between the barnyard and a stretch of bright riffle water. I walked upstream, crossed at the shallows and scanned the pool.

"Tell John to fish the hopper wet. They're taking it. He'll take fish," Jamie said.

John trudged upstream along the bank. He looked like a beat dog.

"I've had this wind knot since you left," he said when he reached us at the stretch of good water. "Can you fix it?"

I cut the leader at the tippet and tied on spiderweb-thin stuff for the rainbows in the sun. When I was done, John began fishing the hopper downstream like a wet fly. The first rainbow that hit jolted John's arm hard; but he had no experience at striking trout rising to a fly, and the fish was gone when he yanked back.

"You yanked the fly away from him. Hold the line between your rod hand and forefinger and press your forefinger against the line and lift all at once when you see the fish strike," I said. "You've got to watch the fly so you see the fish strike before you feel the tug. It gives you that edge you need to hook him." I said it all, knowing that he'd have to learn by doing. I said it just to have something to say while I watched. Jamie told him to cast to the bank and to let the fly swing with the current downstream until it hit the bottom of the swing. He told him to strip-retrieve with the line between his forefinger and the rod so the line would be tight when a trout hit.

"If you strip a little, the line will be tight and you'll be more ready," Jamie offered.

"Oh, there's another one, and I missed him too!" John exclaimed. He kept striking and missing and striking, until he finally hooked a rainbow, and the fish jumped and danced and flipped off at his feet. He was dejected, but not beaten.

My son did not take a trout that fine October day, but I'm sure he learned many of the long lessons of fly fishing. Perhaps the most important lesson he learned was that you can do everything wrong with a fly rod and line and still have fun on a stream. Although he may not have realized it, he also learned that dry flies can be fished effectively wet; that trout lie facing upstream; that they strike hard and spit out the fly very quickly; and I'm sure he learned that your fly casting suffers badly when you get excited. He learned that fly fishing is fun. He learned that it can also be difficult, challenging and all-consuming in its demands on attentiveness.

John began to learn all the things I have been learning about fly fishing since I began on a similar stream at this age (12). I've been at it now for nearly thirty years. I still get the same racing pulse when I see a trout rise. It's still childishly fun and inviting.

Fly fishermen will always invite you to a trout stream to join them in their fun. And David Lee is extending that invitation in this dandy book. I almost said ". . . for beginners." But to be honest, there are no beginners in fly fishing—just those who are finding for the first time what they have missed.

I like to think of fly fishing as the ultimate movable feast of sport. I can carry its degrees of difficulty as far into the sublime as I want, all the way to fine cane rod-making or salmon fly tying. Or I can assume the role of voyeur and travel to exotic streams where the scenery is beautiful and the fish are many and easy to catch. I can become a social fisherman if I choose, fishing the pleasant evening rises and savoring streamside stories over a fine meal in a well appointed lodge. Or I can return to my youthful years—when dunking worms in small brooks for the tug of tiny trout was fun—by fishing small streams with a bright Coachman, catching and releasing trout as I go. I can keep my fish or release them unharmed. And in this choice of kill or not kill I have the ultimate option of sport: I have fooled a fish with my artifice (the fly) and my cunning (the presentation), but having achieved and thrilled to the excitement of the strike and the fight, I release the trout for another matching of wits on another day. Or, I may decide to keep a mess of fish for a fine meal. The choices are mine, and I can make them in the best surroundings—alone.

Although I'm not a snob, I like the people I meet while fly fishing more than people I meet at other sporting events. Fly fishermen seem to thirst for challenge, companionship, achievement without competition, good fellowship, and sport within an unstated code of sportsmanship that might seem quaint in America if it did not have its origins so firmly rooted in history and tradition.

As David Lee reminds us, fly fishing is hoary in its origins. The sport began a long time ago; yet it has a vitality today that has not been chronicled before. Its vitality springs from that delight I saw in my son that October morning on the Mettawee: All humans love to catch fish. The Japanese have discovered fly fishing, and they are rushing to learn the sport with their typical verve. Fly fishing has also become a popular sport in the U.S. and Europe. Who could ever believe such a thing would happen? Fly fishermen were supposed to be doddering old eccentrics who did strange things on streams. Those days are gone forever.

Please take this invitation offered by David Lee's fine introduction to the sport. His advice is excellent in every aspect of fly fishing he discusses. How I wish that this helpful book had been available to me when I first began my fun with a fly rod. It could have sped me that much faster along a chosen path. Catching fish is fun; catching fish with a fly rod is delight.

PREFACE

This book is designed to give you the basic information that you will need to begin the process of becoming proficient in fly fishing. Because so many beginning anglers experience unnecessary frustration, many people believe that fly fishing is an especially difficult sport. It is my hope that this book will eliminate some of that frustration.

The chapters that follow are arranged so that you should find it comfortable to read straight through. If you already know something about fly fishing and want to skip ahead to a topic that interests you, that should be possible too. Each chapter has been written to be a simple but comprehensive introduction to one aspect of the sport.

There are many good books about fly fishing. So at the end of each chapter I will recommend a book or two that can provide you with additional detail on the subject of that chapter. Often you will find that these books offer points of view somewhat different from my own. Controversy abounds in fly fishing, and you will benefit by getting acquainted with diverse views.

Like most highly specialized pursuits, fly fishing has a special language all its own. At the end of the book I have provided a glossary that offers short definitions of the terms that have been introduced and discussed in the preceding chapters. This should serve as an easy reference for mastering some of the vocabulary that fly fishermen use in talking about their sport.

Finally, let me assure you that this book will not make you an expert fly angler; only the fish can do that, and they can be demanding instructors indeed. If expertise is your goal, I hope that you achieve it. More important, I hope that you will find in fly fishing the challenge and pleasure that I have enjoyed in the pursuit of this fascinating hobby.

Acknowledgments

A great many people have had a part in the completion of this book, and I owe them a real debt.

David Barnes, former Prentice-Hall college textbook representative, was instrumental in getting the project off the ground. He believed in the book before I did, and that made all the difference.

My brother Paul and my friends Bill Elliott, Dick Montgomery, Ralph Schmidt, and Bill Wells reviewed the manuscript and made a number of helpful suggestions. Ron Kepple and David Guiney contributed to the photographic effort; they loaned their equipment and gave their expertise with equal generosity.

A number of the companies in the fly fishing industry assisted me by allowing the use of previously published material and by arranging for me to use, evaluate, and photograph some of their products. I am grateful to Dick Gaumer and Fenwick/Woodstream; Tom Rosenbauer and the Orvis Company; Bruce Richards and Howard West and Scientific Anglers; Dick Jennings and Leon Chandler and the Cortland Line Company; Rex Thomas and Alan Carver and Browning; The Russell Moccasin Company; Paul Johnson and Berkley and Company; Guillaume Sacre and the Danner Shoe Company; and Eric Price, vise-maker extraordinary.

Dan Feaser's illustrations have greatly enlivened and enhanced the book. I am grateful for Dan's friendship as well as his talent. John Randolph, Lefty Kreh, Joe Humphreys, Charles K. Fox and Ed Shenk were generous with their encouragement and advice.

Mary Kennan and Fred Dahl, my editors, answered my many questions with patience and advised me well.

My daughter Meg showed understanding beyond her years (6) in tolerating my preoccupation during a long summer when we might have been camping and fishing more often. And the contributions of my wife Katherine to the book are beyond recounting. Photographer, editor, proofreader, advisor; without her, much more than this book would have been impossible.

1
WHAT FLY FISHING IS (AND ISN'T)

If you're like many people just getting interested in fly fishing, you may have only a vague idea of what the sport is all about. In fact, in my experience of teaching beginners how to fly fish, I have met several people who have even fished with fly equipment without being sure what fly fishing consists of or how it differs from other forms of angling.

Also as a beginner, you may feel a little awed by what seems to be a highly complicated sport. That feeling is only natural. A lot of the specialized hobbies that people enjoy seem baffling to those who are not yet initiated into their mysteries. The purpose of this chapter is to eliminate some of the mystery. We'll talk about the basics: what fly fishing is, what makes it different, and how it evolved over many centuries

The essential element in fly fishing, of course, is the fly. The characteristics of the fly dictate all the other aspects of the sport: the tackle, the techniques, the theories, the traditions. It all begins with the fly, and so we will begin there too.

A *fly* is a hook around which has been wrapped some materials (usually fur and feathers), which are intended to represent something that a fish will think is edible. Some flies look more realistic than others, and some are more effective than others, but all of them have one characteristic in common: They weigh very little. So little, in fact, that flies cannot be cast with ordinary fishing tackle.

Typical fishing tackle is designed to cast bait or lures that have significant weight. Whether you are casting a spinner, plug, or live bait, the principle is the same: The weight is thrown through the air, and the fishing line follows it to the target just as if you had tied a string to a rock and given it a heave.

Flies can't be cast this way. If you doubt it, try to throw a fly across the room! This combination of near weightlessness and air resistance limits the distance that a typical fly can be thrown to a few inches. Obviously some other principle has to be involved in fly fishing. In fly fishing, it is the *line* that is cast because the line provides the casting weight. The fly goes along as an extention of the line; it is the passenger on the trip, not the vehicle.

This is why fly lines are so much thicker and heavier than other fishing line and why fly rods are generally longer and have a different flexing "action" from rods designed for spinning or bait casting. This is why casting a fly rod is a different process from casting with conventional fishing tackle.

Although the actual origins of fly fishing are not clear, it seems obvious that at some point a fisherman saw fish feeding on insects, tried to use the insects as bait, found them too fragile, and got the idea of tying materials on a hook as a substitute for the real thing. The would-be fly fisherman soon found it necessary to modify the rest of the tackle as well, and fly fishing was born. We can be certain that those early experiments were successful, for the sport has persisted and spread.

Fly fishing was probably well established by the time of Christ, and possibly much before. The Roman historian Claudius Aelian, who lived in the second century A.D., described Macedonian anglers:

They fasten red (crimson red) wool around a hook, and fix on the wool two feathers, which grow under a cock's wattles, and which in color are like wax. Their rod is six feet long, and their line is the same length. Then they throw their snare, and the fish, attracted and maddened by the color, comes straight at it, thinking from the pretty sight to get a dainty mouthful; when, however, it opens its jaws, it is caught by the hook and enjoys a bitter repast, a captive.

Today the essentials of fly fishing are not much different from Aelian's description. There is, however, much greater variety in the styles and types of flies, and many of these developments are relatively recent. Let's look now at the various types of flies and how they are constructed and fished.

Wet Flies

Wet flies are those that are fished under the surface of the water. Early fly fishing was exclusively wet fly fishing, and it was with the wet fly that the first attempts were made to represent the stream organisms on which fish feed.

In addition to the baitfish present in most streams and rivers, there are also many varieties of aquatic insects. These insects spend most of their lives as underwater creatures, breathing through gills. Then, near the end of their lives, they emerge from the water as air-breathing, winged insects, go through another transformation into sexually mature adults, and return to the stream to mate, lay their eggs, and die. These insects are available to the fish at several of these stages. Historical writings show that even the earliest anglers understood the importance of imitating stream insects and designed their flies to do so.

Figure 1–1
A traditional wet fly

The earliest references to fly fishing in English appeared in *A Treatyse of Fysshinge with an Angle*, published in 1496. The author was Dame Juliana Berners, an English nun who was the abbess of Sopwell. Dame Juliana noted that stream insects emerge in a reliable seasonal pattern, and she recommended twelve flies, one to be fished in each month of the year.

Wet flies much like those recommended by Berners appeared again in Izaak Walton's classic *The Compleat Angler* in 1653. Walton himself was primarily a bait fisherman, and the impact of his book on fly fishing was greatly increased when Part II was added to the fifth edition in 1676. This section, entitled "Instructions How to Angle for a Trout or Grayling in a Clear Stream," was written by Charles Cotton, a young angler who had become a friend and fishing companion to Walton. Cotton expanded the list of flies to sixty-five patterns, several for each of the most productive months in the year.

The flies described in these early writings resemble a number of wet flies still in use, and the general style of wet fly construction has not changed much in five hundred years. The typical wet fly has a tail of soft feather fibers, a body of fur with perhaps a contrasting ribbing, a wing of more feather fibers, and a "hackle" or rooster neck feather, wound on edge and slanted toward the tail of the fly.

Many modern anglers like to fish two or three wet flies on one leader. In ancient times it was common to fish as many as a dozen wet flies, strung out along a horsehair line. This practice, along with the fact that these anglers had no reel but simply tied the line to the end of the rod, may account for why Dame Juliana recommended rods of eighteen feet in length!

Many theories account for the effectiveness of wet flies. Fish may mistake them for immature stream insects, drowned land insects, or even small baitfish. Whatever the reason, wet flies still work.

3

Dry Flies

The *dry fly*, as the name implies, is designed to float on the surface. These flies were developed to imitate the stage of aquatic life when the winged insect emerges on the surface. The first mention of a fly specifically designed to float appeared in 1836, and by 1850 many British anglers were fishing with dry flies regularly.

An Englishman, Frederick Halford, did the most to popularize dry fly fishing. Unfortunately, he also encouraged the belief that dry fly fishing was the only proper method of fly angling. Halford and his followers believed that a gentleman would use only dry flies, he would cast his fly only to a visible, feeding fish, and only in an upstream direction.

Figure 1–2
A dry fly tied "Catskill" style

Halford's flies traveled to America in response to a request from a New York angler named Theodore Gordon. Gordon, suffering from tuberculosis, had given up a promising career in finance to retreat to the healthier climate of the Catskills. He modified some of Halford's flies to suit American conditions, invented some new ones of his own, and American dry fly fishing was born.

Gordon's "Catskill" style of dry fly is still widely used today. It incorporates a divided upright feather wing, a slender body of stripped quill or fur, a tail of stiff hackle fibers, and a collar of the same stiff hackle, for supporting the fly on the surface of the water.

The enthusiasm of Halford and his followers changed fly fishing tackle and techniques in fundamental ways. Rods became shorter and stiffer, because dry fly anglers often needed to switch the fly back and forth through the air ("false casting") to flick excess moisture off the fly. And anglers became more interested in entomology and the precise imitation of stream insect life.

Nymphs

Nymphs are a specialized form of wet flies, tied specifically to imitate the immature stages of aquatic insects. Most nymph flies have a tail of soft feather fibers, a fur body to represent the abdomen of the insect, an enlarged forward portion to suggest the "thorax" of the natural nymph, and a collar of soft hackle to suggest legs.

Figure 1–3
An artificial nymph

Nymph fishing was pioneered by G. E. M. Skues, a British angler who risked (and received) the outrage of Halford and his fanatics when he published *Minor Tactics of the Chalk Stream* in 1910. Skues' crime was in suggesting that a sportsman could fish for trout with a submerged fly, something no dry fly purist would admit. Many English fishing clubs would not admit anglers who fished with nymphs, and Skues and his critics exchanged heated articles in the sporting magazines. The trout, however, proved Skues right. In most waters, fish consume 85 to 90 percent of their food below the surface, so the nymph angler is presenting them with something apparently edible under much more favorable circumstances than the dry fly fisherman.

Today most anglers try to be skilled with both the dry fly and the nymph, as well as the wet fly, and many have come to agree with Skues that nymph fishing is more difficult than dry fly fishing ever was. In fact, today there is something of a "nymph cult," almost as exclusive and fanatic as Halford and his followers in their day. Fishing techniques may change, but human nature endures.

Streamers and Bucktails

Strictly speaking, streamers and bucktails are not flies but lures. They are designed to imitate small fish rather than stream insects. Nevertheless, since they are fished with the fly rod, tied by fly tiers, sold in fly shops, and taken by the same fish that strike wets, nymphs, and dry flies, these minnow imitations are always included when flies are discussed.

Bucktails are made of hair, often but not always the hair from the tail of a deer. *Streamers* are constructed of feathers, usually tied arching back over the hook shank in a fish-like profile. Both varieties are manipulated in the water so that the undulations will represent the swimming motions of a forage fish, especially one that is injured or otherwise vulnerable.

Figure 1–4
A streamer

Some streamers are just elongated versions of famous wet flies. In other cases a fly may be designed to represent a particular baitfish known to be an important food source of the game fish being sought. Although streamers are a relatively recent development in the history of fly fishing, there is evidence that some primitive peoples developed streamer-like lures, although they did not use other fly fishing techniques.

Most fly anglers use streamers and bucktails regularly. They are particularly good flies for beginners to fish with, because almost any technique of fishing them can be effective. They are also effective during high water and for night fishing.

Most importantly, streamers and bucktails are big fish flies. A large majority of the trophy fish caught on flies are taken on baitfish imitations, simply because large fish need large meals and because the streamer fisherman is offering just that. A few fly anglers fish with them almost exclusively, on the theory that big fish can be taken on dries, wets, or nymphs only under certain conditions, but they may attack a baitfish imitation at any time.

Until recently, fly fishing meant fishing for trout. Some say that the trout was designed for fly fishing, and few would argue that point. Quite probably, though no one knows for sure, the first fish caught on a fly was a trout. Nevertheless, over the years many other species of fish have become objects of the fly anglers interest.

The ultimate fish for the fly angler is the Atlantic salmon. British fly fishers discovered the joys of fly fishing for salmon centuries ago, and it remains the peak experience of many fly anglers. Sadly, the Atlantic salmon fishery has been severely harmed by the pollution and damming of the freshwater rivers, to which the salmon return to spawn, as well as by the decimation of salmon schools at sea by commercial fishing. As a result, Atlantic salmon fishing is now greatly diminished and expensive, available only to the few.

While the Atlantic salmon fishery has declined, West Coast anglers have pioneered in fly fishing for Pacific species of salmon as well as

Figure 1–5 A gentleman angler of the nineteenth century

6

the steelhead, a rainbow trout returning to fresh water to spawn after a period in the salt. Unfortunately, the Pacific fishery faces many of the same problems that have threatened the salmon fishing of the East Coast.

Fly fishing for bass is one of the most rapidly growing aspects of the sport. Largemouth bass, found in rivers, farm ponds, and large impoundments, are sought most often with fly rod bass bugs, especially during spawning and during their shallow water foraging periods. The smallmouth bass is an even more popular fly rod fish, although it is less widely distributed. Like the trout, the smallmouth prefers swift streams with rocky bottoms and feeds freely on insects. Even more than the trout, the smallmouth is an explosive and tenacious battler, and its tendency to jump when hooked endears it to fly rodders.

The members of the sunfish and panfish family are also good quarry for the fly rod fisherman. Bluegills in particular are fine fly rod fish, and they can be caught readily on dry flies and nymphs. A husky bluegill turning its side to the current can put a good bend in any freshwater fly rod and make for a downright thrill on light tackle. Not only are these panfish available in most parts of the country, but their fine eating qualities make them a favorite of fish lovers. And unlike many other fish sought by the fly rodder, they reproduce so rapidly that they can be taken home in large numbers with a clear conscience.

Saltwater was the last frontier of the fly rod, and it is now well explored. Tarpon, sailfish, marlin, and many other saltwater species have fallen to the long rod. While saltwater fly fishing usually requires specialized tackle, some saltwater species can be taken on trout equipment. No wonder that saltwater fly fishing is growing in popularity so rapidly.

Today the opportunities to fish with the fly rod are more diverse than ever before, more so than anyone could have imagined on that long-ago day when the first trout found a hook in its jaw when it meant to eat an insect. But the essence of fly fishing is the same as it was then. Fly anglers seek to understand the fish's world, so they can participate in it well enough to fool a fish into eating an artful creation of fur and feathers with a hook hidden inside.

In this book, our emphasis is on trout fishing and, to a lesser degree, on fly fishing for bass and panfish. These fish are the ones that beginners want to catch, and they are also the fish that are most available to most people. Once you learn to catch these fish on flies, then moving on to fish for other species or to saltwater fly rodding is mostly a matter of changing equipment and mastering some new and specialized techniques.

In the next few chapters we'll get you outfitted for fly fishing, practice your casting stroke, build a vest full of accessories, and teach you some knots that you'll need once you're on the stream. Then it will be on to the fishing and on to learning how to use flies to catch the fish you want to catch.

Recommended books

Trout Fishing by Joe Brooks (Harper & Row, 1972). This is perhaps the best book by the late master angler and writer. The emphasis is on fly fishing, and the chapter on the history of angling is one of the most complete anywhere.

Fly Fishing for Trout: A Guide for Adult Beginners by Richard W. Talleur (Winchester Press, 1974). This is a superb beginner's book for those interested strictly in trout fishing. Talleur based the book on his course in fly fishing originally developed for Trout Unlimited classes. It is comprehensive yet straightforward. If you decide to read another beginner's book (and I recommend that you do), put this one at the head of the list.

2
FLY FISHING TACKLE

For the length of your rod, you are always to be governed by the breadth of the river you shall choose to angle at; and for a Trout-river, one of five or six yards is commonly enough, and longer, though never so neatly and artificially made, it ought not to be, if you intend to fish at ease, and if otherwise, where lies the sport?

Charles Cotton
From Walton and Cotton, The Compleat Angler *(1676)*

Charles Cotton wrote those words more than three hundred years ago. But if he could spy on you on the stream today (and I for one would not guarantee that he can't), he would recognize instantly that you were fly fishing. Moreover, if he could borrow your equipment, he could probably master the use of it with only a few minutes of practice.

Fly fishing tackle has changed during the two thousand years or so of the sport, but the changes have been evolutionary rather than revolutionary. Today's rods, for example, are only about half as long as those Cotton used and recommended. Our modern fly lines are of plastic rather than of braided horsehair or silk, and our leaders are of nylon monofilament rather than silkworm gut. These, however, are changes of form, not function.

9

As you know, the characteristics of fly tackle are determined by the flies themselves. In fly fishing, since the flies do not have enough weight to be cast with conventional fishing tackle, it is the line that is cast, and the weight of the line is distributed along its entire length rather than concentrated at a single point. Everything in fly fishing begins with the fly.

Your decisions about tackle should begin with the fly too. Beginning fly fishermen often purchase the rod first, then a line and a reel, and then decide what sort of flies to use. This process almost always results in frustration because, to handle properly and cast well, the line, leader, fly, and rod must all be in a harmonious, balanced relationship to each other. You can achieve this balance by making your decisions in the following order:

1. Decide which types of flies you will use most often.
2. Based on that decision, select a fly line of appropriate weight and taper.
3. For that line, select a rod of ideal length for your conditions.
4. Then select a reel with enough capacity to hold the line and to complement the rod.

Let's examine these decisions one at a time.

Selecting a Fly Line

Begin by deciding on the type of flies you will fish with and where you will be fishing them most often. As a beginner, you may find the decision difficult, and you may benefit from consulting an experienced fly fisherman in your area. If you are unable to locate such a person, the following guidelines will help you.

Line Weight

Remember that in fly casting the line is cast, because the line provides the necessary weight. But different stream situations require lines of different sizes, and different rods require lines of different weights to bring out the casting actions designed into them. So lines are manufactured in a variety of weights to reflect all these differences in fishing situations.

At one time, fly lines were identified by their diameters, and letters of the alphabet were used to designate the various sizes. This system made putting together a balanced outfit extremely difficult, because, as we have seen, the weight of the line is critical, and the system provided no way to relate weight and line diameter. So even if you had a rod that the manufacturer indicated was to balance with a D line, you could not be assured of good casting performance because D lines were not standardized with regard to weight, only diameter. A D line from one maker might work fine; another from a different company might work miserably. When lines were designated in this way, only experts had a reasonable chance of assembling a well balanced outfit without a lot of expensive and frustrating trial and error. No doubt many people gave up on fly fishing before ever getting to the water.

Some years ago the tackle manufacturers, urged along by some committed fly anglers who wanted to simplify things for the beginner, adopted a new system for fly line standards based on the weight of the first thirty feet of the line as indicated by a number. The numbers run from 2 to 15; the higher the number the heavier the line. What the numbers mean in terms of actual weight is indicated in Table 2–1, but you don't really need to know the actual weight of your fly line. The number associated with that weight is the essential piece of information, and with that you can select a rod that will cast it properly.

Table 2–1   American Fishing Tackle Manufacturers Association Fly Line Standards

Number	Weight*	Range
1	60	54–66
2	80	74–86
3	100	94–106
4	120	114–126
5	140	134–146
6	160	152–168
7	185	177–193
8	210	202–218
9	240	230–250
10	280	270–290
11	330	318–342
12	380	368–392

*Weight is in grains (437½ grain = 1 ounce) and is based on the weight of the first thirty feet of the line, exclusive of taper.

As a beginner you will probably be considering lines in the weight range of 5 to 8 or 9. Lines of 4-weight and lighter are for extremely delicate fishing conditions involving tiny flies, extra-long leaders, clear waters, and sophisticated fish. Chances are you won't be facing conditions like these right away—at least not as a steady diet. Lines of 10-weight and heavier are used primarily in saltwater fly fishing, and the real heavyweights are designed not so much for casting ease as they are to balance rods that are strong enough to fight big saltwater fish.

Beginning fly fishers seldom go wrong by selecting a line in the middle of the freshwater fishing range; that is, 5-, 6-, or 7-weight lines. Here are my recommendations, expressed in terms of line weights:

LIGHT WEIGHT LINES. If you expect to be fishing very small flies often, if you will seldom need to use weighted flies, if most of your casts will be fifty feet or less, and if you plan to fish where high winds are not often a problem, a 5-weight line will meet your need to present the fly delicately and still provide a moderate degree of versatility.

MEDIUM WEIGHT LINES. If you expect to fish flies in all size ranges, with an occasional need to fish weighted flies, and if your fishing is done on waters of moderate size and flow, the selection of a 6- or 7-weight line would be appropriate. The 7-weight is probably the most versatile of all line sizes; with it you can fish weighted streamers in heavy water or cast small dry flies over finicky trout. The 6-weight is almost equally versatile, but it sacrifices some of the wind-fighting punch of the 7-weight for an increase in delicacy.

HEAVY WEIGHT LINES. If you will be fishing large rivers, if you will often use weighted flies, or if you live and fish where wind is often a problem, an 8- or 9-weight line will suit your needs. The 8-weight is the better of the two from a presentation standpoint, but if you intend to fish a lot of large bass bugs or make an occasional trip for light saltwater angling, you will find the 9-weight more suitable.

If I had to select only one line for all my personal fishing, it would be a 6-weight. Most of my angling friends, if pressed, would choose a 7-weight. If you face commonplace conditions, one of those two will probably meet your needs.

Line Taper

Now that you have the basics of line weight, you must consider another variable: taper. Fly lines are available in several taper configurations: level, double taper, weight forward taper, bug or saltwater taper, and shooting taper (also called "shooting head.")

THE LEVEL LINE. The level line is the least expensive. It is the same diameter all the way from one end to the other. Because it is not tapered, it does not present the fly with the delicacy of a tapered line, nor does it cast as well under most conditions. For these reasons, level lines are not favored by most experienced fly anglers. Like most inexpensive things (unfortunately), level lines do a fair job but not a superior one.

THE DOUBLE TAPER LINE. The double taper line is probably the most popular fly line for all-around fishing. At each end, this line is tapered to a fine diameter where the leader is attached (see Figure 2–1). This taper makes for smooth casting and a soft presentation of the line, leader, and

Level

Double Taper

Rocket Taper

Bug Taper

Salt Water Taper

Shooting Taper

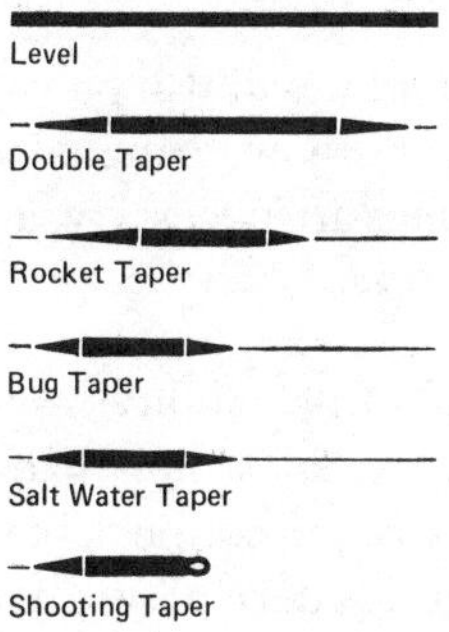

Figure 2–1
Modern fly tapers (Courtesy
the Cortland Line Company)

fly on the water. The double taper is much more expensive to buy than the level line, but with the same taper at both ends the line can be reversed when one end becomes worn, so the double taper is not much more expensive to use. The double taper is also a good line to use when a lot of false casting and roll casting are necessary (more about those casts in Chapter 3).

THE WEIGHT FORWARD LINE. The weight forward taper line has become very popular in recent years. This design concentrates most of the weight of the line in the first thirty feet. This *head* or *taper* is the portion of the line designed to be cast by the rod. The remainder of the line is called the *running* or *shooting* line; small in diameter, it will shoot through the rod guides easily and follow the head to the target, making longer casts possible.

When weight forward lines were first introduced, they were not highly regarded by trout fishermen because the front tapers were too *steep*; that is, they sacrificed delicacy for distance. In recent years, though, weight forward lines have been redesigned by most manufacturers, and most of them now have exactly the same taper as a double taper line of the same size. This modification has increased the delicacy of the lines and led to their increased popularity.

Weight forward lines are not without disadvantages. They are not reversible, so they lack the economy of double taper lines. Then, too, the angler must keep in mind that the first thirty feet of the line is the portion that can actually be cast. If the angler attempts to hold more than thirty feet of line in the air the cast will break down because the small-diameter running line is not heavy enough to support the head in the air. In practice this is no great disadvantage, but it does take some getting used to, especially for anglers used to double taper lines. Nevertheless, there is a growing consensus that the increase in distance that the lines afford outweighs their small disadvantages. I fish with them most of the time now, and most of my friends do too.

There is a special variety of weight forward line called the *bug taper* or *saltwater taper*. These lines are designed with much steeper front tapers, so the weight is heavily concentrated in the front portion of the line; this feature makes these lines relatively easy to cast long distances. Delicacy, of course, is sacrificed, but that is not necessary in the bass bugging or saltwater angling where these lines are used.

THE SHOOTING TAPER LINE. A final specialized line you may encounter is the shooting taper or shooting head. This is nothing but the taper of a weight forward line without any running line included. Anglers who must repeatedly make long casts, like Western steelhead fishermen, attach small-diameter fly line or even flat monofilament to the back end of these tapers and hurl them across wide rivers. Shooting heads are superb under such conditions, and more anglers are turning to them when casting distance is a prime concern.

Line Function: Floating, Sinking, or Both?

Your first fly line should be a floating line, and it will still be your basic fishing line long after you have become an experienced angler. At the same time, there are occasions when sinking lines are necessary, and a great variety is now offered by line manufacturers.

FLOATING LINES. Today's basic fly line is a marvel of floatability, especially when compared with the silk lines of yesteryear. Those lines had to be greased repeatedly to make them float, and they required special care in between fishing trips to keep them from rotting. Modern plastic lines require little care except for occasional cleaning, and they are designed with air bubbles trapped in the line so they float all day with no special effort on the angler's part. Floating lines are the basic lines in fly fishing. They are used not only to fish surface flies but also to handle streamers, wets, and nymphs in waters of moderate depth and current.

SINKING LINES. These lines, which sink from one end to the other, represent the oldest form of sinking line and have been available in many line weights for years. More recently, line makers have made available lines of different sink rates for use in various depths and current conditions. There are many types: if you're interested, the catalogs of the manufacturers can provide detailed information. Keep in mind that you should select a sinking line with a sink rate appropriate to your conditions. Again, advertisements and catalogs are good sources of information on the various types of sinking lines, as well as on the conditions for which they are intended.

FLOATING-SINKING LINES. A few years ago, *sink-tip* lines were introduced. These lines were made so that the first ten feet sank and the remainder floated for better visibility and line control. These lines were so good for getting the fly down into waters of moderate depth and current speed, that they were soon followed by lines with twenty feet of sinking tip, and then thirty feet. Today all these are available in a wide range of line weights, sink rates, tapers, and fluorescent colors, too.

INTERMEDIATE LINES. These lines are designed to deliver the best features of the old silk lines that anglers cursed for so many years. (Their good features were easy to overlook in light of all the care they required.) These lines float when dressed with a silicone paste, and they sink just below the surface when not dressed. They also have a harder finish and somewhat smaller diameter than floating lines in the same sizes, so they have a different casting "feel," which some anglers find superior to ordinary floating lines. They are especially good when extremely subtle presentation is required. If you are going to have only one line, you might do well to consider an intermediate. They are extremely versatile.

Color

Today's fly lines are available in just about every shade of the rainbow. Traditionalists favor somber lines of brown, gray, or off-white, but there are some good reasons for considering the bright lines. For one thing, bright lines can help improve your casting because they make it easy to watch your line in the air and to correct casting faults. They also make it easier to follow your fly, and this is especially important when you're fishing with an extremely small or submerged fly.

Some argue that brightly colored lines scare fish, and I'm sure that's true if you're careless enough to show it to them. A line of any color will spook a fish if cast over its resting place, but it is the disturbance on the surface that alarms the fish, not the color of the line. In fact, the color of a floating line is hard to detect from below the surface; all lines look dark against the sky. The trick is to keep the line away from the fish. If you do so, it won't matter what color it is.

A System for Line Selection

Now you know the four variables you must consider in choosing a fly line: weight, taper, function, and color. The next question is: How do all these variables get sorted out in the store? Luckily, the line makers have agreed on a system explaining their fly lines and what they do. The system is based on letters and numbers, with the letters defining the taper and function and the numbers indicating weight. Color, of course, is visible through the package.

First in the designation are the letters to indicate the taper (or lack of it):

- L = level
- DT = double taper
- WF = weight forward (Some weight forward lines are further described as "bug" or "saltwater taper" on the package.)

Then comes the number indicating the weight of the line. Following that, more letters indicate what the line does:

- F = floating
- S = sinking
- F/S = floating with a sinking forward portion (If you want to know

how much of the front section sinks, you have to look on the box for more information. Most manufacturers call a line with a ten-foot sinking section a *sink-tip*, one with a twenty-foot sinking section a *sink-taper*, and one with a thirty-foot sinking portion a *sink-belly* or *sink-head*).

Here are a couple of examples of the system as it appears on a fly line box:

WF6F weight forward floater, 6-weight
L7S level sinking line, 7-weight
DT5F double taper floating line, 5-weight
WF9F/S weight forward 9-weight line, floating with a sinking front portion

One final word about fly lines. I have learned from experience that this is one place where you cannot afford to economize. You'll find that the major line makers are competitive in their prices, and you can get some discount by ordering through catalogs. But fly lines that are markedly cheaper than those you order by mail are likely to be quite inferior and not worth the money, no matter how cheap they are. I've probably wasted fifty dollars trying to buy a good five-dollar fly line, and as far as I can tell, there is no such animal. No part of your equipment is more important than the fly line, and nothing can compensate for poor line performance. Put your money in a good fly line, and you won't be disappointed.

Selecting a Fly Rod

Once you have settled on the line, you can start looking for a rod to cast it. If you know other fly fishermen, you will have no shortage of advice. All the fly anglers I know love rods, and they love to talk about them, argue about them, fish with them, and (to the dismay of their spouses) buy them. You will find partisans on every side of every fly rod controversy: long rods versus short rods, bamboo versus graphite, glass versus bamboo, and so on and so forth.

As with lines, you must consider many things when selecting a fly rod. First, of course, is making sure that you select a rod to properly cast the weight of fly line that you have chosen. Most commercially available fly rods have the line weights they are designed for printed on the shaft, just above the hand grip. You will find many different rods that will cast the line you have in mind, so you will need to consider some additional variables before making a final choice.

The function of the rod is fairly simple: It acts as an extension of your arm and allows extra leverage in the casting stroke. If you've ever seen a real expert give a fly casting demonstration, you know that a really super caster can throw a fly line with no rod at all, although I don't know of any who would want to fish that way.

The rod makes casting easier not just because it extends your reach, but because it resists bending. The weight of the fly line bends the rod, but the rod resists the bending and springs back to its original straightness, imparting power into the cast and catapulting the line through the air. So the rod extends the angler's leverage, it bends, and then it straightens again. The coming together of these functions on the stream is the measure of rod performance.

Fly Rod Components

Let's examine the parts of a fly rod, so you know what to look for when you shop. You may wish to examine Figure 2–2 as we look at the various components that make up a rod.

The heart of the rod is the *rod blank*. The quality of the materials and the accuracy of the taper of the blank contribute heavily to the quality of the rod as a casting tool. You can examine the rod shaft closely to look for flaws, but essentially you must trust manufacturers for blank quality. You can get good clues, however, from the quality of the fittings. If the other components are cheap, the chances are that the blank is not of high quality either.

The very last guide at the top of the rod is called the *tip-top*, or *tip guide*, for obvious reasons. On most fly rods the other guides are made of wire and are called *snake guides* because of their shape. The guide closest to the hand grip will probably be what is called a *stripping guide*, that is, a ring guide much like the type you may be familiar with on spinning or bait casting rods. On some high-quality rods, this stripping guide is made of carborendum or ceramic, because much of the friction of the line during casting is concentrated on this lowest of the rod guides. On some newer rods, all the guides are small ceramic ring guides, but most rods still have snake guides except for the stripper and the tip guide.

In guides, you should look for two things: number and quality.

Figure 2–2 A typical two-piece fly rod

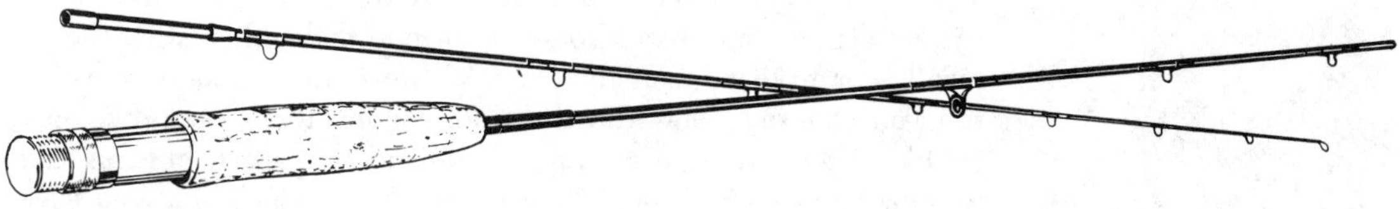

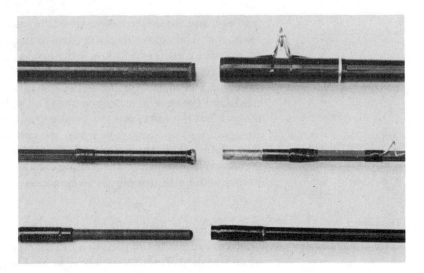

Figure 2–3 Three types of ferrules. *Top:* A glass ferrule on a Fenwick rod. *Middle:* A nickel-silver ferrule on an Orvis split-bamboo rod. *Bottom:* An internal-spigot type ferrule on a Scientific Anglers graphite rod. (Photo by Katherine G. Lee)

Avoid rods with guides that have been obviously painted or plated gold; the soft metal hidden underneath will soon abrade that expensive fly line. The best snake guides are hard chrome-plated. Beware of a rod with too few guides. A manufacturer of cheap rods can save a lot by dropping a guide here and there, but a rod with too few guides will not perform well because the fly line will slap against the blank, and the friction will impede the cast. As a rule of thumb, a rod should have at least as many guides as it is long in feet, and one more than that isn't too many. It is also true that a rod can have too many guides, but you're not likely to confront that in a mass-marketed rod.

The small wire guide just above the hand grip is called the *keeper guide.* It's for parking your fly when you're not fishing, so don't string the line through there!

The joint where the sections of the rod fit together is called the *ferrule.* Ferrules of nickel silver are used on high-quality bamboo rods, as well as on a few graphite and boron models. Most graphite and glass rods of good quality have gone to another ferrule system, usually one in which the lower part of the blank fits into the upper portion. Metal ferrules are to be avoided on inexpensive rods; they not only ruin the casting action, but they also soon corrode and either stick the rod together or make it difficult to set up. Whatever the ferrule system of the rod you choose, follow directions for joining them carefully. Some ferrule systems require twisting to join and take apart, but this same twisting will destroy others. Be sure you know which kind you have.

The hand grip may be made from many different materials, but all the fishermen I know prefer cork. Chances are you will too. The *reel seat* is the last fitting at the lower end of the rod, and it is an important one. Some reel seats lock in an upward direction, and some lock down. I prefer the up-locking type, because as I fish, the heel of my hand seems to work down the rod grip a little, loosening the locking rings on a down-locking seat. Whatever the system, make sure that the hoods for the reel feet fit the reel you intend to use, and look for a seat with two locking rings rather than one. Although one locking ring is sometimes resorted to on light-weight rods, on rods of medium weight the additional locking ring makes for much greater security for your reel, and the additional weight is not important.

Look for good fittings, carefully assembled. A manufacturer who skimps on components is not looking for business from serious fishermen.

Fly Rod Materials

Today the fly angler has a choice of rod materials far broader, both in price and characteristics, than ever before. Let's consider some of the variables.

Figure 2–4 A variety of hand grip and reel seat styles. *Top:* A down-locking metal seat on a South Bend glass rod. *Second from Top:* A down-locking seat with walnut spacer on an Orvis bamboo rod. *Third from Top:* An up-locking cork seat on a Fenwick graphite rod. *Bottom:* A down-locking cork seat on a Browning boron rod. Note the wide variation in rod blank diameter between glass, bamboo, graphite and boron. All these rods cast a 6-weight line (Photo by Katherine G. Lee)

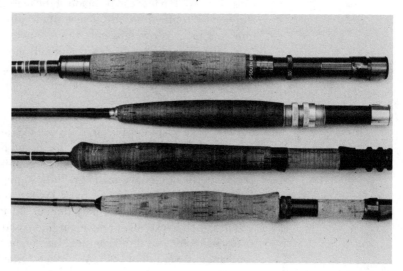

GLASS. Glass rods have been widely available to American anglers since shortly after World War II, and they have been improving all the time. The modern glass fly rod is a durable piece of equipment that will give years of trouble-free service with a minimum of maintenance. And the best glass rods of today handle a fly line as well as the best rods of any material only a few years ago. Glass rods are the least expensive rods available to the fly angler, although the very best of them can be quite expensive. Possibly, however, you can find a real bargain in a glass rod now that graphite rods are coming down in price and competing with them. As with the fly line, you will do well to put your money into the product of a reputable manufacturer. If you can talk with more experienced anglers about your choices, so much the better.

GRAPHITE. Graphite, a product of carbon fiber technology, has been available in fly rods since the early seventies. Originally developed for specialized applications in the aerospace industry, graphite fibers have extremely high strength for their weight. They also have what engineers call a "high modulus of elasticity," which means that graphite resists bending and returns to straightness rapidly after flexing. These properties combine to make a superior fly rod, in which light weight, high power, and a good casting "feel" are all combined. Graphite rods also have a smaller diameter than either glass or bamboo rods, so they offer higher rod speed and less air resistance to the casting stroke—an important consideration if you fish for long periods at a time.

Graphite rods became very popular with fly fishermen almost from the moment of their introduction. Most anglers feel these rods give them more distance in their casting and more comfort as well. The light weight of graphite has contributed to the revival of the long rod, since rods of nine or ten feet can be made of the material without making them feel cumbersome or clubby. I recently acquired a graphite rod that is nine feet long, yet weighs only three ounces!

Although graphite rods are generally more expensive than glass fly rods there are some exceptions. A couple of major manufacturers have introduced graphite rods that compete favorably in price with glass rods of good quality.

BORON. Like graphite, boron is a space-age material that has recently been available in fly rod blanks. Some boron rods are a combination of boron fibers and graphite, and others are all boron. Boron has most of the properties that have made graphite so popular, only more so. It is lighter than graphite, has an even higher modulus of elasticity, and makes for a rod that is extremely slender. I have used a boron rod that was designed to cast a 7- or 8-weight line, yet it was smaller in diameter than a ballpoint pen at the handle. Many of the boron rods now available can handle several line sizes. While most graphite rods can cast a line one size heavier than designated by the manufacturer, some boron rods will balance with four or even five line weights.

So far, boron rods have found such favor with anglers that their manufacturers can't keep up with the orders. They are quite expensive, however, and it remains to be seen if the small advantages they offer over graphite rods are worth the large difference in price.

BAMBOO. The history of the last century of fly fishing is largely a history of fishing with split-bamboo fly rods. Late in the nineteenth century, American craftsmen discovered the benefits of bamboo cane over the varieties of wood then in use, and, for the first half of this century, practically all fly rods were made of bamboo. Some of these rods were so fine that they are worth thousands of dollars today; other cane rods sold for a few dollars when new and are worth little more today.

Bamboo was an ideal material for fly rods not only because of its casting properties, but also because it was cheap and so was the labor required to turn it into a rod. Things are different now. The countries where the best cane is grown were once colonial possessions, but they are now independent nations located in some of the most unstable parts of the world. And we all know what has happened to labor costs!

It takes about a month to assemble and finish a split-cane fly rod. The best bamboo for rod building is a species named Arundenaria amabilis. It grows in the Gulf of Tonkin region of China and northern Viet Nam. Once it is imported, the best poles are selected, split, and then milled into strips according to the tapers required for the particular action of the rod being built. A number of these strips (usually six, although five- and seven-strip rods are occasionally encountered) are glued together to form the rod blank. Then the guides, reel seats, and grips are installed, and the final finishing steps taken. No wonder that an average cane rod can cost several times as much as a good graphite rod. Cane rods cost in the hundreds, occasionally thousands, of dollars.

Are they worth it? Most anglers who fish with bamboo will tell you that nothing really equals the "feel" of cane action. They often have trouble putting these feelings into words, but when you fish with a cane rod, you may find that you agree. Remember too that a modern cane rod is an example of some of the finest craftsmanship remaining in this mass-production economy. Finally, check the used rod lists. You'll find that most cane rods are appreciating in value. If you take care of a bamboo rod, it should never be worth less than you paid for it and will probably be worth more someday.

Cane rods, however, are not without their disadvantages. I don't feel comfortable fishing weighted flies or sinking lines with a fine bamboo rod because high stresses can put a bend, or "set," in the delicate tip sections. Careful casting is also required. If a fly hits the rod at high speed, the hook may dig into the finish and actually damage some of the fibers underneath. At the very least, the rod may require some minor refinishing after such an accident. In a word, fine cane rods require more care and maintenance than rods of artificial materials. Cane rod lovers think they are worth the extra trouble; others do not.

Whatever your rod purchasing decision, you would do well to put off considering a fine cane rod until you have gained considerable experience in fly fishing. Not only will you select your rod more wisely then, but you will also have acquired the finesse to appreciate the subtle, but real, benefits of bamboo.

Rod Length

Like the hemlines of women's skirts, fly rod length is subject to the whims of fashion. There are objective factors to be considered, of course, but subjective and personal considerations play a large part in length preference. Let me use two good friends as examples:

Terry Ward was a student in a psychology class I taught about eight years ago. I knew about psychology, whereas Terry knew about fly fishing; the result was that our roles as teacher and student were soon reversed. Terry taught me generously and well, and I have never fished with him without learning something new.

Terry lives in the Cumberland Valley of Pennsylvania, home of some of the most famous trout streams in the country. A few years ago, Terry pulled a ten-pound, four-ounce brown trout from the waters of the Letort Spring Run, and that fish is still one of the largest trout ever caught in Pennsylvania. Since then, although not neglecting fish of moderate size, Terry has become a specialist in big fish, and regularly yanks trophy-sized browns, rainbows, and brook trout from the fabled waters near his home. On our most recent trip together, Terry netted a twenty-four-inch brown trout and an eighteen-inch rainbow in the space of about twenty minutes.

Terry accomplishes these miracles with a rod that most anglers would say is too short by half. When I first fished with Terry he was using a Fenwick glass rod, five feet in length. On our most recent trip, he used an Orvis graphite of about the same length, a one-piece rod designed to cast a 4-weight line. With such a rod you might suppose that Terry is limited to fishing small flies, yet he regularly tosses weighted streamers half the size of your fist with this outfit. Terry feels that his short rod allows him to cast with greater accuracy, and it also allows him to poke his big streamers into the snag-surrounded holes that big trout like to inhabit. Whatever the rationale, you can't argue with success. Terry's short rod works for him.

Bob Abraham represents the other end of the spectrum. Bob was raised in the Catoctin Mountains of Maryland, and he still lives there, close to the headwaters of Big Hunting Creek. As a boy, Bob used to fish

Figure 2–5 Terry Ward and his Letort monster. The trout is nearly as long as the rod Terry uses! (Photo by Ed Shenk)

his way down the mountain to school in Thurmont, hide his rod under some brush, and then fish his way back home again after school. Rumor has it that he skipped school altogether when the trout were hitting.

Today, Bob works for the Maryland Department of Natural Resources, and few men devote their time more generously to beginning fly fishers than Bob Abraham. Like Terry Ward, Bob was one of my teachers in fly fishing, and I'm still learning from him whenever I get the chance.

Bob favors a relatively long rod for this fishing, and his pet for Big Hunting Creek is an eight-foot Fenwick glass rod that carries a 6-weight line. Bob feels strongly that his rod allows him much better control of his line and fly, with less effort, than would a shorter rod. Bob also tries to avoid wading when possible, because it tends to alarm the fish and disturb the water for anglers who may follow. The long rod lets him stay out of the water most of the time. As Bob says, "With three feet of arm and eight feet of rod I can reach all the way across the stream in many places." With such a reach, Bob feels he has a system that gives him the control he needs with minimum disturbance of the water and the fish. Like Terry Ward, Bob has found a method that works for him.

23

Figure 2–6 Bob Abraham tests a new rod on wintry Big Hunting Creek. (Photo by Katherine G. Lee)

The proper conclusion to draw is that the skill of the angler counts for a lot more than the size or type of the equipment. I have no doubt that Bob and Terry could catch trout with broom handles and binder twine. Still, as a beginner, you would be wise to select your first rod from somewhere in the middle of the length spectrum. You will develop preferences as you gain experience in fly fishing, but, as with the fly line, you will not be sorry if you avoid the extremes in the beginning.

What all this means in terms of rod length is about seven and a half feet. Such a rod is long enough for good line control, and short enough to be handled well even on brushy or overgrown streams. If you plan to fish often from a boat, or to fish in situations where long casts are the rule, then eight and a half or even nine feet might be best. If you will fish small trout streams exclusively, and if these are densely grown up with brush, you might want to go as short as seven feet. But for most occasions, you will not go wrong matching your 6- or 7-weight line to a rod of about seven and a half or eight feet.

Rod Action

Today's fly rods are considerably more standardized with regard to rod "action" than was once the case. Still, some variation remains, and anglers often have preferences for one rod action or another.

Generally speaking, a rod is considered to have a *fast* action if most of the bending takes place near the tip, say in the last third of the rod's length. A rod that bends down into the midsection has a *medium* action, and a *slow*-action rod bends all the way down into the grip. At one time, anglers selected rods for the type of fishing they intended to do. It was said that dry fly fishing called for fast-action rods, and wet fly fishing for slow-action rods, and so on.

Most of today's rods are medium-action rods. To assess the action, you really need to cast the rod with the line attached. But with a glass or bamboo rod you can estimate the action by holding the rod with both hands about waist high and whipping the tip smartly to one side or the other. By noting how far the bend runs down into the rod blank, you can estimate the rod's action characteristics. Boron and graphite rods cannot be assessed in this way; they are too light to flex themselves and must be loaded with a line before their true action can be evaluated.

More important than action—for my money at least—is the stability of the rod. When you flex the rod, watch the tip closely. It should *dampen*, or stop vibrating, rapidly after only one flexing. The tip should oscillate in the same plane, that is, back and forth in the same straight line, rather than in an oval configuration. A rod that vibrates in an eccentric fashion tends to throw waves into the cast, and that is highly undesirable.

As you must have detected by now, rod action is a somewhat subjective topic, like the personal considerations that go into the selection of rod length and material. With all these subjective factors involved, you should arrange to actually cast with an outfit before you buy it, if at all possible. The better fly tackle shops expect customers to want to try rods, and many of them have casting facilities. Testing a rod is more difficult to arrange if you buy from a department or discount store. Good fly shops also have experienced sales people who can help you select matched equipment (you'll find a list of such shops in Appendix B.) You are unlikely to find such expertise in department or hardware stores.

Building Your Own Rod

If you're a beginner, it probably hasn't occurred to you that you could assemble your own rod from a kit and thereby acquire a fine rod at a very reasonable cost. Most of the major rod makers supply their products in kit form, and you can save a bundle by providing the labor yourself. Rod building is quite easy, and it provides additional satisfaction for anglers who enjoy doing their own custom work. Most of the catalogs listed in the Appendix contain rod kits as well as books on rod building. Your local library probably has a book on the subject too.

Developing some rod-building skills might make it possible for you to acquire a bamboo rod without a major investment. Sometimes good used ones are available that can be returned to service with minor repairs and refinishing. Often, also, repairable old cane rods can be found lying around basements and attics.

Recently my mother-in-law gave me an old cane rod her father had fished with, a rod that I estimate to be around seventy-five years old. I refinished it (not a major job if you read up on it first) and replaced the guides and other components. When I was finished I took the rod and a selection of lines to my yard in high anticipation. I was sorely disappointed from the very first cast. The old cane had lost heart. It was weepy and limp even when loaded with my lightest lines. Then, on impulse, I detached the lower third of the rod and tried casting with just the midsection and the tip. It felt a lot better, so I stripped the midsection again, replaced the snake guides with a single stripping guide, and fashioned a hand grip and reel seat out of cork rings. I now have a delightful small stream trout rod, six feet in length, that handles a 4-weight line beautifully. The butt section, with the old reel attached, decorates my mantel; the rest of the old rod is going into battle again.

Ordering from a Catalog

If you plan to order a rod from a catalog (and there are often good financial reasons for doing so), you should arrange to try out a rod like the one you intend to order. Even if you don't know other fly anglers yet, you could probably arrange to test a rod much like the one you are interested in by contacting a local sportsman's club and requesting assistance. Your chances would be especially good if you can locate a nearby club affiliated with Trout Unlimited or The Federation of Fly Fishers. However you make the arrangements, you would benefit by casting with several rods before settling on the one that suits you best. I'm sure you will find the local anglers cooperative. After all, any excuse to talk about rods, argue about rods, cast with rods . . .

Fly Reels

Some say that a fly reel is nothing but a place to store line. Like many other generalizations, this one is true except when it isn't. Most fish caught on flies, at least in freshwater, are played with the line (usually the left) hand. Nevertheless, when you finally hook a trophy fish that takes line from the reel, you won't want to lose it to a cheap reel.

You can buy a decent fly reel with a good drag system for a reasonable sum. You can also spend a fortune for a simple fly reel, especially if you choose one of the British reels made of exotic alloys. In the high-priced reels you are paying for light weight and high craftsmanship, and you can keep right on paying for it up to a hundred dollars and even beyond. These things are desirable, no doubt about it, but they are also things you can sacrifice with no loss in fishing effectiveness. An inexpensive reel will serve you well if you choose it with care and take care of it. A cheap reel can cost you a fish that you really want to land.

The most common fly fishing reel is the *single-action reel*. This reel has a simple spool with an attached handle; one revolution of the handle equals one revolution of the spool. In most of the fly fishing situations that you will encounter, nothing more complex is required, and the single-action reel has the advantage of being simple, light-weight, and relatively trouble-free.

Multiplying reels, on the other hand, contain a gear mechanism that produces more revolutions of the spool than revolutions of the handle. These reels may be needed by anglers who fish big water and who make long casts repeatedly or by those who fish for species of fish that are capable of stripping off a lot of line that the angler may have to recover in a hurry.

Automatic reels are also available. Working by a spring mechanism, the reel slurps up the fly line automatically when the fisherman presses a button. I don't use automatic reels, and I don't know many serious fly anglers who do. These reels are heavy and complicated,

Figure 2–7 A selection of single-action fly reels. *Clockwise from Top Right:* Berkley Specialist, Cortland Crown, Scientific Anglers "System" by Hardy Brothers of England, Cortland Graphite. The Berkley and Cortland Crown reels are popularly priced. The Cortland Graphite is in the middle-priced range. The Scientific Anglers reel is one of the more expensive. All except the Cortland Graphite have exposed-rim spools for adding drag with the palm. (Photo by Katherine G. Lee)

and they have no room for adequate backing (described below) behind the fly line. Most of them have rough drag systems that cannot be adjusted to work reliably with light leaders. The only situation in which an automatic reel might be desirable is in fishing from a boat, where the reel can rapidly recover line that might otherwise clutter the deck and foul around an obstacle. I don't think this small advantage outweighs the faults of the automatic reel, but you might feel differently.

Most good-quality reels, single-action or otherwise, are available with extra spools. This feature is extremely desirable, since it enables the angler to carry extra fly lines (such as a sink-tip) without buying and carrying another entire reel. Be sure that the reel you select has extra spools available and that your dealer actually has them on hand when you need them.

Backing

Remember to buy a reel that has enough capacity to hold a line of the size you intend to fish with, along with some backing. *Backing* is small-diameter fishing line, ideally of dacron, that builds up the spool diameter of the fly reel while protecting the angler from the run of a really big fish. Obviously, on small streams the line length needed for a run isn't really a consideration, but the spool diameter always is. Building up the diameter allows you to take in more line with each revolution of the spool handle, and it minimizes the kinks that tend to occur in the portion of the fly line closest to the core of the reel.

Install your line and backing as follows:

1. Fasten and wind on your line with the front taper going on first, so that the end of the line that you don't intend to fish with is the last to go on the spool.
2. Then attach backing (check the chapter on knots) and continue to fill the spool to within about a quarter-inch of the reel pillars.
3. Then unwind everything, attach the backing to the spool, and wind the backing and the line back onto the spool again.

This seems like a lot of trouble, but it is the only method that assures the maximum backing the first time unless you buy a reel that comes with a chart showing how much backing of a certain test can be accommodated with each line size and taper.

You will note that double taper lines take up more reel space than weight forward lines of the same weight. The running line of the weight forward line is a small diameter, while the double taper line is thick throughout, except for the short tapered sections on either end. With the weight forward line you can use a smaller, and therefore lighter, reel. You will want to keep this characteristic in mind when you purchase your new reel.

Balance

At one time anglers paid a lot of attention to "balancing" the rod with the reel; indeed a lot of beginning anglers think that this is what is meant by "balanced" fly tackle. Today balancing the rod and reel is not a major concern for most anglers. Most fishermen feel that the lighter the reel the better, especially since many of today's rods are lightweight. The next time you're casting on the lawn, take the reel off and lay it on the ground while casting; you'll see how nice it is to have no reel at all. For this reason, some anglers go to the extreme of cutting a double taper line in half or trimming off the back end of a weight forward line, in order to fit the line on a reel that would ordinarily be far too small.

Which Side to Wind On?

Most reels can be set up to wind from either the right or left side, and many anglers who are used to spinning equipment prefer to wind with their left hand. They argue that, with this system, the same hand that casts the rod plays the fish and that, once the fish is hooked, they don't have to transfer the rod from hand to hand. I have no argument with that system, although I do not use it myself. I started off winding with the casting hand, and I have never felt the need to change. Had I started winding left-handed, I would no doubt be just as satisfied.

Drags

Most single-action reels provide some sort of drag system, primarily to prevent the spool from overrunning when line is stripped off by the angler or a running fish. I prefer to set the drag as light as possible; in fact, I often figure out how to set it even lighter than the maker intended, by bending the springs that hold the drag pawl against the reel spool rachet.

A light drag is desirable for a number of reasons. First, of course, on some occasions you play fish of moderate or large size on very light leader tippets. If the drag cannot be set very light under these conditions, the fish breaks off as soon as it runs line down to the reel. Second, many anglers do not realize that the effective pressure of *any* drag setting is increased as line is payed out, because the drag is working against a spool of rapidly decreasing diameter. You can lose a fish if the drag is set too tightly to begin with. This is another reason why backing is so advantageous: By helping to fill the spool to capacity, it helps to keep the actual working drag reasonably light. Finally, a light drag setting is desirable because it is much easier to add drag, while playing a fish, than it is to reduce it. You can add drag with your fingers, by pressing against the interior of the spool, against the line or against the outside of the spool as it turns. Nothing is more delicate or more rapidly adjusted than finger pressure that you apply yourself.

Many of today's reels are made with an exposed spool rim for adding drag with your fingers or palm. One thing to keep in mind about exposed-rim reels is that some of them do not lend themselves to left-hand winding. When the line is stripped from the reel, it tends to drag across the exposed rim of the spool if the spool is faced in the same direction as the line of pull. Although the rim edges are not really sharp, they are abrasive enough to rapidly wear a fly line that is repeatedly dragged across them, because the rim is turning, like a saw blade, as the line is pulled past it. If you decide to set up an exposed-rim reel for left-hand winding, train yourself to pull line off the reel straight down.

In summary, then, you will want to look for a single-action reel, inexpensive but of reasonable quality, and fill it with the line of your choice plus whatever amounts of backing you have room for. Then set the drag as lightly as possible, just tight enough to prevent spool over-running. Most of the time, as the saying goes, your reel will just be storing line. But when you need more from it, you will be able to count on a good performance.

Leaders

Like the other parts of the fly flinger's gear, leaders can get complicated. We'll keep the leader description simple to start with and wait until a later chapter to go into more detail.

The leader's function is twofold: First, the leader separates the fly from the line; second, it delivers the fly to the target. For both purposes, the leader must be tapered. The *butt* end of the leader must be large enough to approach the size and stiffness of the fly line, so the energy of the cast can be transferred into the leader. The other end, called the *tippet*, must be small enough to attach the fly, and the fly may be small indeed. The transition from the butt end of the leader to the tippet is called the *taper*.

Like a lot of subjects in fly fishing, there are many opinions about how leaders should be designed. Many anglers tie their own leaders, experimenting with different formulas, lengths, and leader materials.

For getting started, you can do nicely with chemically tapered leaders. These are the ones that taper without knots, and they are available in all fly shops and many sporting goods stores. They are sold according to length and X designations. (I'll explain later how X" corresponds to pounds test and diameter, but you don't need to know that to get the right leader.)

I would recommend that you buy two leaders to begin with. Make one of them about seven and a half feet, tapered to 3X, and the other nine feet or so, tapered to 4X. Along with them, pick up small spools of leader material in 3X, 4X, 5X, and 6X. (If you're wondering why you should buy more material in 3X and 4X after purchasing leaders in that size, the reason is that, once you clip off and tie on several flies, a 3X leader, of the knotless taper type, isn't 3X anymore.) With this small investment in leaders, you should be able to get by for a season. After that, you'll know whether or not you want to start making your own.

Summing Up

Now you know something about lines and rods, reels and leaders, and perhaps you'll make a more informed choice when the time comes to buy. Might I make another suggestion? Think about your choices for a while, and let your ideas kind of "settle" a bit before you rush out and buy that first outfit. I know this advice is easier to give than to follow, and I don't want to dampen your enthusiasm. But you will find that getting to know some fly fishermen in your area is helpful, and so is familiarizing yourself with the tackle stores nearby.

In the Appendix at the back of the book is an extensive list of fly shops around the country. Each of these shops (and many others like them) have expert personnel who are qualified to help you try out and select equipment suitable to your needs. Also listed in the Appendix are a number of mail-order distributors (some of them have retail stores too) of top-quality fly tackle, materials, and books. Many more are in business than are listed, but I have chosen to include those that I have actually dealt with myself. I can vouch for their quality and service.

Each of these firms will send you a catalog on request. If you become a subscriber to one of the major fly fishing magazines, you may get the catalogs without asking for them. Many of these mail-order firms will sell you a complete and balanced fishing outfit for a package price somewhat lower than the price of all the components purchased separately. And most of the catalogs contain useful information for beginning fly fishers, so you can learn something from them as well.

Good luck in your tackle hunting. Once you assemble your outfit, we'll get together for some casting practice.

3
FLY CASTING

There are many memorable sights in sports: the staunch point of a good bird dog, the graceful pivot of a second baseman turning a double play, the leap of a wide receiver for a touchdown pass. Certainly high among these is the sight of a good fly caster exercising his or her skill.

Indeed, it is the casting that attracts many people to fly fishing. I remember clearly the first time I saw the art in practice. Although I had fished all my life, none of my tutors were fly fishermen, so I reached late adolescence without knowing much about the sport. Then, on a college outing to a lake in central Pennsylvania, I saw a fly angler. He was casting to rising trout, and he landed several, but his equipment and his method of using it captured my interest.

I suppose I must have seen fly casting somewhere before that day, but never just as I saw it then. The long rod raised, slowly at first and then with increasing speed. A sudden pause sent the line arching past the rod tip and looping far behind the angler, straight as an arrow. Then just as the line straightened to the fullest, the forward stroke began and started the line moving in the other direction, moving with gathering speed, until it rocketed past the caster, turned over, and set the fly down on the surface as delicately as a snowflake.

Right then I decided to try fly fishing for myself. I could already catch fish, at least sometimes, but now I wanted to catch them in this new way. Indeed, I wanted to learn to cast with a fly rod, whatever the result; the fact that fish could be caught in the bargain was a bonus.

If you are like the typical person just getting started in fly fishing, you probably feel about casting much as I did nearly twenty years ago. Like me, you may be a little apprehensive about trying to learn a skill that seems so graceful and delicate. Let me assure you: Fly casting is beautiful to watch, and it is graceful and lyrical, a sheer joy just to do, but you don't have to be beautiful, graceful, or lyrical yourself to master it. Anyone can learn to cast successfully, by investing a little time and by being willing to make the necessary effort.

My experience with beginning fly fishermen suggests that they often hold contradictory ideas about fly casting. At first they think that fly casting is so difficult that they can never master it. Then, once they start to practice, they become rapidly impatient with their progress. Actually, the level of difficulty in fly casting falls somewhere in between these two extremes. Casting is relatively simple, but it is new to most people. And some of them, particularly those who have used other types of fishing tackle, have to unlearn some old habits before their casting progresses rapidly.

Fly casting, then, is relatively easy to master at a satisfactory level of competence, but it requires many hours, even years, of practice to achieve excellence. This very characteristic makes so many sport skills, from golf to skiing, so fascinating. We can learn them rapidly enough to put them into practice in a short time, and yet we can always improve our skill, no matter how many years of experience we have.

I think that fly casting intimidates most beginners a little bit, especially if they have seen a real expert at work. But you need not be intimidated by fly casting, as long as you allow yourself the time to learn properly and have the same patience with yourself that you would offer to another beginner learning a skill that you already practice well. Let me suggest a few things to keep in mind as you begin to practice your fly casting:

1. *Be patient.* Give yourself time to master the skill. Few people learn to cast well rapidly, and real expertise requires years of fishing experience, most of which isn't planned but just happens. Take your time and enjoy yourself while you're learning.

2. *Set reasonable goals.* Many people who are reasonable about most things are not very reasonable in the goals they set for themselves in fly casting. I once had a fellow in my fly fishing class who wanted to learn to cast like the great Lefty Kreh. Ordinarily I wouldn't quarrel with such a noble objective—I'd like to cast like Lefty myself. The trouble was that this guy wanted to do it overnight! This same fellow could

undoubtedly dribble a basketball a little, but if somebody had suggested to him that, with a little practice, he'd be as good as Walt Frazier, he'd have laughed at the idea. And yet, as I tried to point out to him, his goal in this case was just as unrealistic. Lefty Kreh is a fine athlete, blessed with razor sharp reflexes and terrific timing. And he had something else too. I once asked Lefty to what he attributed his incredible casting skill. Without a moment's hesitation he replied, "Bass bugging on the Potomac River . . . twelve hours a day." The casting skills of the greats like Lefty, Jim Green, Leon Chandler, and the rest are useful to us as models of casting at its best, but they do not represent what most of us, who are limited by time and athletic skill, are capable of.

3. *Don't work too hard at it.* Fly casting will probably call into play some muscles that are not used to being exercised. You will tire fairly quickly at the beginning, and if you keep practicing with tired muscles you will start to favor them and develop poor form. It's better to practice frequently for short periods of time than infrequently for long periods.

4. *Fly casting does not require strength, but timing.* If you find yourself working hard, you're not doing it right. The movements that

Figure 3–1 A great fly caster in action—Lefty Kreh (Photo by Irv Swope)

make up a good fly cast are quick movements, but they are not hard ones.

5. *Don't worry about distance at first.* I'm not going to tell you that being able to cast a long line isn't an advantage; it is. But it isn't something that should be a priority for you at the beginning. I doubt that you will follow that advice, but it is good form to give it. So there it is.

I don't know why it is, but I have never known a beginner, myself included, who didn't want to fling the fly line into the next county, right off the bat. Even experienced anglers want to cast farther than they can, no matter how far that is, because they know that distance casting can be an advantage in many fishing situations. We all want to do it, and I'll bet you'll be no exception. Remember, however, that straining for distance will tire you faster and promote poor form. Also, your concern for long casts leads you to attempt to muscle the fly line through the air, and that's sure to frustrate you as well as impair your casting stroke. So fight the urge to cast too far too soon.

6. *Concentrate on accuracy and a soft delivery of the fly.* Accuracy is the most critical variable in fly fishing. Your first cast to a fish is the money cast, and all the succeeding ones have a rapidly diminishing likelihood of success. The time you spend straining for distance would be better spent learning to put the fly where you want it the first time. If you can hit an area the size of a pie plate at thirty feet, you will catch more than your share of the fish. And if you can do this with a soft delivery, you will be more successful than most of the anglers on the stream today.

7. *Be prepared for some frustration.* Psychologists know a good deal about acquiring skills, and one of the things they have learned is that most people experience what's called the "plateau effect." That means that you will probably make pretty good progress early in your training, but then reach a point where you seem unable to improve no matter how hard you try. Plotting this phenomenon on a graph shows this period of frustration as a plateau between two upward curves of improvement. What can you do about the plateau effect? Not much, except to recognize it for what it is and persevere. It will end, and, when it does, you will start to make strong progress again. And this time you will be moving toward real expertise.

The Mechanics of Fly Casting

Now let's talk about the actual casting. But there's a problem: Nobody I've ever known could *think* about all the things you're supposed to do in order to cast, and *actually cast* a fly rod at the same time. We analyze casting with our brains, but we do it with our hands, arms, wrists, and so on. The act of analysis is intellectual, while the act of casting is a psychomotor performance.

Another factor, too, makes the transition from analysis to performance difficult. When we talk about a skill, or draw it, or diagram how it's done, we almost always break it down into small bits of the overall performance and look at these bits individually. The act itself, however, is all one thing. The discrete bits that we diagram actually flow together so that no one can tell when one ends and the next begins. And if you try to practice them as if they were a series of independent movements, you won't end up with the skill you want. You'll have a series of herky-jerky motions that don't resemble the flowing reality of the skill.

So, I'm going to try to analyze a fly cast for you, and at the end of the chapter, I've recommended a couple of the very best books on the subject. But, as you probably know, most people who are really good at something learn to do it first, and then explain it later. Great fly casters are no exception; first they get to be great, and then they stop and figure out what they do that makes them great. This is why fine casters don't agree on what makes fine casters, and why there is so much individual variation or "style" in the performance of any skill.

Someone once asked Yogi Berra, the great Yankee catcher, if he hit with the trademark up or down. "I go up there to hit, not read," said Yogi. The story may be apocryphal, but the point is valid: Understanding a skill to the fullest is not essential to superb performance, and many experts do what they do without much analysis. The opposite is also often true. I know anglers who can describe a perfect fly cast but who can't cast a lick.

Nevertheless, let me describe some of the mechanics of casting, so that you can think about them before you practice, even if you can't think about them while you practice. Remember that the weight of the fly line makes fly casting possible. The caster moves the rod, and the weight of the line resisting that movement bends, or *loads*, the rod. The rod resists the bending, however, and soon straightens again, launching the line through the air. This process happens once on the backcast and once again on the forward cast.

The caster controls every part of the cast by adjusting the movement of the rod: the distance, speed, and, most important, timing of the movement, as well as the pauses between movements. The pauses between rod loadings actually cause the loop in the fly line that is so characteristic of good casting. This loop, rolling through the air, carries the power through the line and delivers the fly to the target. A good illustration of the movements, pauses, and their consequences in the loop formation is shown in Figures 3–2 and 3–3.

All of the rod action comes together at the tip. The starting and stopping of the rod tip is the critical act in casting, because this forms the loop and because the quality of the loop determines the quality of the

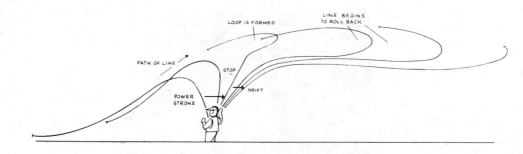

Figure 3–2 The back cast (Courtesy Fenwick/Woodstream)

cast. If you recall only one aspect of this analysis, remember this: The line does what the tip dictates. Tip movement is critical to good fly casting. You could say that fly casting consists of learning to make the rod tip do what you want it to do from your position at the other end.

A Practice Session

Let me describe a typical casting practice session, much like some of those that you will have soon. In the course of the practice we can describe what a good cast is like, as well as what can go wrong.

Your yard is an excellent place to practice most of the basic casts. If you have water nearby, so much the better. But using the yard will make it possible to practice frequently with little bother, so I'll assume that's where you are.

String up the rod, and pull about twenty feet of line out past the tip (that's twenty feet in addition to the leader). Stretch this line straight out on the grass in the direction you want your forward cast to go. Now go back to the rod, pick it up, and hold it comfortably in your hand, preferably with your thumb on top of the grip. With your other hand, grasp the line as it comes off the reel and strip enough line until your two hands are a comfortable distance apart, say, a foot or two. Now, just hold

Figure 3–3 The forward cast (Courtesy Fenwick/Woodstream)

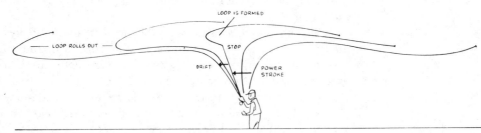

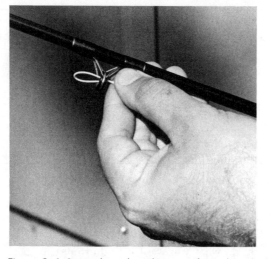

Figure 3–4 String the rod up this way. If you drop the line, the loop will open and prevent the line from falling all the way through to the ground. (Photo by Katherine G. Lee)

the rod in this position for a few seconds and feel comfortable with it. When you are ready to cast, begin, but don't rush yourself.

First make the backcast, and that will blend immediately into the forward cast. To begin the back cast, lower the rod tip, point it toward the end of the line, and take up any slack line in your line hand. Now, in a smooth motion, begin to lift (not jerk) the line off the grass. That's it, nice and smoothly. As all the line except the leader clears the grass, power the rod (but don't overpower it) in an upward direction, flexing it so the line is propelled up and behind you. If you can imagine a large clock face beside you, the power stroke of the backcast should begin at 10:30 or 11 o'clock and end at 1 o'clock, as shown in Figure 3–5.

Ending the backcast power stroke causes the loop to form and the line to roll out behind you. Wait until the line has almost completely straightened before beginning the forward cast. The forward cast stroke is made in the same power zone, between 1 o'clock and 11, as shown in Figure 3–6. When you stop the rod this time, the loop forms in the other direction, the line rolls through the air, turns over, and delivers the fly to the target.

If you're anything at all as I was on my first attempt to fly cast, the line is now piled at your feet, quite possibly tangled around your neck, and you're wondering how you got into this mess in the first place. Let's examine what you probably did wrong. After all, since you're only reading and not really casting, you won't take these remarks personally.

First, you probably jerked the line off the grass rather than lifting it smoothly, so that it had already leaped toward you and was falling away

Making the back cast

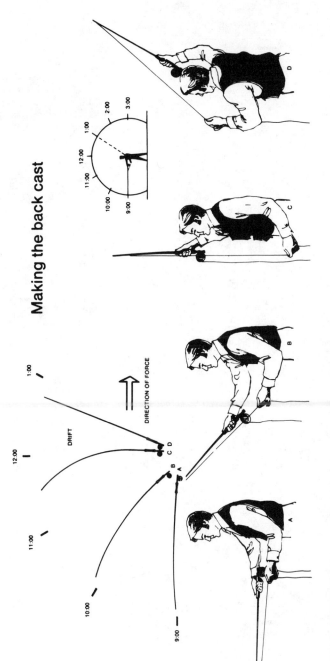

Figure 3–5 The back cast in detail. Note the rod positions as related to the imaginary clock face. (Courtesy Scientific Anglers)

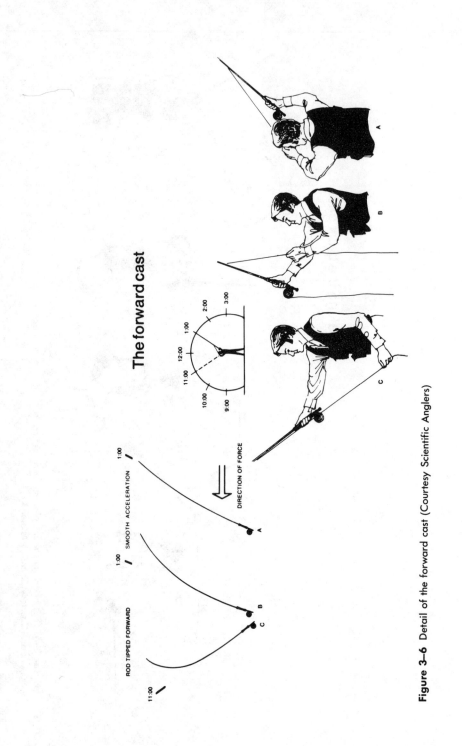

Figure 3–6 Detail of the forward cast (Courtesy Scientific Anglers)

again. So when you started the power stroke on the backcast, you were exerting your power against a slack line. Then, to compensate and try to save the cast, you overpowered the backcast stroke, which made the rod tip bounce and threw more waves of slack into the line. Following that attempt, you carried the power stroke too far back, well past the imaginary one o'clock position, with the result that the backcast became a down cast and hit the ground behind you. Then, when you started the forward cast (undoubtedly too soon or too late), you were again exerting power against a slack line. You probably overpowered the stroke again, and you carried the rod tip too far down, so that you pulled the bottom out of what little loop there was and destroyed the cast. That's how the line got around your neck.

Actually, if these problems have really happened to you, all it proves is that you are exactly like just about everyone who has started to learn to fly cast—and the huge majority of those folks are now casting well and catching fish. What I have tried to do is to describe an ideal fly cast and then show what can often go wrong with it at first. I think you can learn to do it properly faster if you can recognize a poor cast and the causes of it.

Another Approach

Now let's look at the same process from another viewpoint. As indicated earlier, all the good books on fly casting are written by experts who learned to do it first and who then explained how to do it. I have a theory that this same approach will work for most people, so I'm going to describe what the product of good casting is like and urge you to focus your practice on achieving that product, rather than on thinking exclusively about the movements that are supposed to bring it about.

A good fly cast always has two essential elements: (1) a tight loop and (2) a straight line. By "tight loop" I mean that the loop formed by the tip is small and narrow; thus it cuts through the air with little resistance and turns over firmly at the end of the cast. The line is "straight" in the air because the cast is generating sufficient line speed to hold it there. On some occasions in fishing, a big loop and slow line speed are needed, but you can always produce these once you have learned the basics— tight loops and straight lines.

Let me offer a few suggestions on how to make a fly cast that has these two elements. Note that these suggestions do not tell you which movements to make but instead describe conditions you can arrange that will help promote the proper movements naturally.

1. *Always practice with a fly attached.* Although flies don't weigh much, they do offer some air resistance to the cast, and you should get used to this feeling from the beginning. Another advantage of practicing

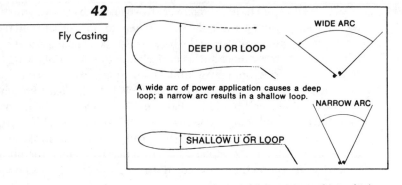

Figure 3–7 Loop control (Courtesy Scientific Anglers)

with a fly attached is that you are forced to practice with a leader attached as well. Failing to do so not only greatly reduces the realistic value of your practice, but it promotes the rapid wear of the end of your fly line. A fly of size twelve is about right, wet or dry. With a pair of cutter pliers, cut off the bend and the barb, everything below the tail of the fly. You now have a practice fly that won't hook you or catch on the grass.

2. *Watch your line in the air*. The quickest way to learn to time the backcast is to watch it. The best way to learn loop control is to see your loop. It may seem awkward to turn and watch the fly line go behind you on the back cast; if so, position your body so that you are standing sort of sideways to the cast, so that you can look easily in both directions. In time you will learn to gauge your timing by feel, but that feel will develop most rapidly if you turn your head and watch your line.

3. *Use a brightly colored fly line*. The brightly colored lines now available are ideal for beginners who need to watch their lines in the air. Even experts can benefit by checking their lines and loops, and these colored lines make it possible to do that under all sorts of conditions. Don't worry about scaring the fish. As you know by now, you should avoid showing your line to the fish, regardless of its color.

4. *Practice your casting stroke with false casts*. A *false cast* is a repeated back-and-forward cast that is not allowed to fall but that is kept in the air with the loop moving back and forth. False casting, of course, requires repeated execution of the casting stroke, and that's why I recommend it. Now, I think that most anglers false cast too much when they're actually fishing (the fish, after all, are in the water). But I don't think you can false cast too much when practicing, because the false cast can tell you almost everything you need to know about your casting stroke.

If your line will not stay straight in the air in both directions, then either your timing is faulty or you're trying to handle a longer line than your present level of skill can support. If your line loop is wide and sloppy, then you are moving the rod tip through a wide arc instead of through a straight line, and you're applying power outside the eleven to one o'clock power zone. But if your line is straight in both directions and your loop is tight, *then whatever you are doing is right!* Keep it up for as long as it is comfortable, and let your muscles get the feel of those motions that are producing the result that you want.

A few years ago, a book by Swisher and Richards (recommended at the end of the chapter) included several casting hints that helped me so much I'd like to pass them along to you. Like the other ideas I have offered here, these tips don't really tell you what to do. Instead they offer ways to evaluate the product of your efforts and to think about the casting process in new ways. First, if you can find a straight line to compare your cast with, you will be able to improve it rapidly. There should be something in your practice area that can serve as a straight edge; a level power or telephone line, the roofline of your house, the top rail of a nearby fence. As you practice false casting, try to "paint" your line along this standard, matching the levelness of your line to the guide.

Another hint is to imagine that you are holding a two-headed hammer, with which you are driving one nail behind you on the back cast, and another in front of you on the forward cast. Obviously, you can't drive a nail straight unless you swing the hammer head in a straight line, so this imaginary hammer promotes good tip technique. If you are casting a short line, then imagine that the two boards into which the nails are being driven are close together. If you're handling more line, imagine them as being farther apart. For example, if you are casting about thirty feet of line, imagine that you are standing sideways in a door frame driving nails into each side of the frame, one in front of you, one behind.

5. *Think about fly casting when you're not actually practicing.* It might sound a little silly, but I think I have improved my own casting simply by imagining and planning my own improvement during some quiet time when I'm not actually casting at all. Think of a good fly cast, even a perfect cast: tight loops in both directions, level line, high line speed, accurate and delicate delivery of the fly to the target. Most importantly, *imagine yourself making this cast!* The more securely you can get this picture imbedded in your mind, the more natural it will seem to do it just that way in reality. Doing so sounds a little mystical, I guess, but I believe it helps you become a better fly caster. Remember that in mastering any skill you must at some point bring together an analytical grasp of the task with the muscle movements required to produce it. Maybe by thinking about the good fly cast, you are preparing your brain to instruct your muscles to actually produce a good fly cast.

To review, then, these few hints should improve your casting rapidly:

1. Always cast with a leader and fly.
2. Use a high visibility line and watch it faithfully.
3. False cast a lot while working to achieve a tight loop, and a straight line.
4. Think about good casting form when you're not actually casting.

Special Casts

Most anglers soon learn that the traditional back-and-forward cast cannot be used under many stream conditions. Sometimes, for example, obstructions behind the angler rule out the normal backcast. At other times, fishing situations dictate a cast that isn't straight or one delivered from the opposite side of the body than is usually the case. Let's examine some of these special casts.

THE ROLL CAST. The roll cast is one of the most useful casts to master. On many streams, in fact, it is used more frequently than the traditional cast. And in some cases, when trees or other obstructions behind the fisherman preclude a normal back cast, it is the only cast possible.

To execute the roll cast, your line must be in the water (the surface tension of the water clinging to the line is what makes the cast work), and you must have some fly line on the water in front of you. Raise the rod slowly toward the vertical, and the line will move toward you on the surface until an arc of line hangs down from the rod tip at a point close to your elbow. At this point, power the rod tip forward and then stop it just as you would in a normal forward cast. The line will roll forward across the water, lifting the fly into the air and delivering it to the target. See Figure 3–8 for details.

In roll casting, as in every other variation of basic fly casting, the behavior of the rod tip determines the cast. If you power the tip too far forward, the line roll will collapse before the fly moves any distance. If you aim the plane of the cast higher than normal, you can roll the entire line into the air, and then execute a normal backcast. This is called the *roll cast pickup*, and you will use it on occasion. Again, it is helpful to imagine that a nail is to be driven into a wall right in front of you—drive the hammer straight, and stop quickly once the nail has been firmly struck.

If you fish weighted flies you will use the roll cast often, because it allows repeated casting without whipping the flies past your ear so often. And sinking lines have to be rolled to the surface before they can be easily drawn from the water for a normal backcast.

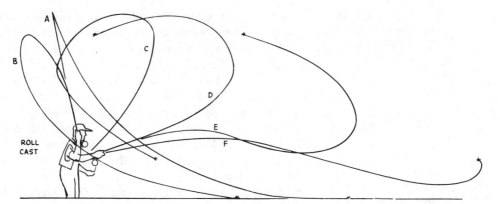

ROLL
CAST

A. Rod is raised to vertical position.
B. Rod is allowed to drift past vertical and stopped so that line hanging from rod tip falls just to the rear of the caster's elbow.
C. Wrist is opened, forward cast is begun with gradually accelerating motion.
D. Full power is applied, wrist is closed gradually.
E. Stop hard, with final added flip.
F. Line rolls out to its destination.

Figure 3–8 The roll cast (Courtesy Fenwick/Woodstream)

THE SNAKE CAST. This one is also called the "S" cast because it involves throwing intentional slack into the cast so the fly is not pulled across the current in an unnatural manner. If you cast a fly to a fish across the stream from you, the current tends to pull the line downstream. In turn, the line pulls the fly across the flow in such a manner that the fish will probably be alarmed. If you throw a lot of waves into the line, you may prolong the free float of your fly.

Remember that the line does what the rod tip does. So you simply "shiver" your casting hand just as you complete the power stroke on the forward cast. The line follows the tip, waving from side to side, and falls on the surface in a series of undulating curves.

THE "SPLAT" CAST. Under ordinary conditions you need to avoid slamming the fly down hard on the water, but in some situations this technique can arouse smashing strikes. For example, when fishing bass bugs I often splash them down fairly hard to create the impression that something edible has fallen in from a streamside tree or bush. When trout fishing, it is often effective to fish terrestrial imitations, such as grasshoppers and crickets, in this way. To make the splat cast, just make the forward cast with more power than necessary and pull the rod tip back toward you just as the leader turns over, thus making the fly turn over and hit the surface with a juicy splash.

THE BACKHAND CAST. This is nothing more than an ordinary cast made
45 across your body, so that what would usually be the back cast goes to the

front and what would ordinarily be the forward cast goes to the rear. Some stream situations dictate the backhand cast. For example, I frequently fish a stream that can only be approached from one side, and from that side the current flows from my right to my left. Since I am a righthanded caster, if I wish to fish this stream in an upstream direction and if I want to avoid splashing my way right up the middle, many of my casts must be backhanded. Most people have little difficulty executing the basic backhand cast, but accuracy is more difficult. Most of our practicing involves working for accuracy on the forward stroke, while the backhand cast requires accuracy on the backcast stroke. So practice the backhand before you need it.

An alternative to the backhand cast is the cast with your off hand, in my case the left hand. Give this a try too while you're practicing. Like the backhand cast, the problem with the off-hand cast is not so much the basic execution as it is placing the fly where you want it.

Of course, many other special casts are sometimes useful. There's the double-haul, the steeple cast, the curve cast, among others. But the beginner is best served by being encouraged to practice a fundamental casting stroke. It's important to learn proper habits early, and you'll do that best by keeping the stroke simple.

Troubleshooting

You will no doubt have some casting problems from time to time, and this list of common problems and their probable causes might help you to analyze and correct them.

1. *Backcast hitting the water behind you:* This is caused by:
   a. carrying the backcast power stroke back too far;
   b. insufficient line speed on the back cast;
   c. waiting too long to begin the forward cast power stroke; or
   d. with a weight forward line, adding running line to the back cast (casting more than the thirty feet designed to be cast).
2. *Knots in the leader:* Although these are called *wind knots*, they are usually caused by:
   a. tipping the rod forward before beginning the power stroke on the forward cast; or
   b. greatly overpowering the forward power stroke. This may also cause the fly to collide with the line.
3. *Snapping the fly:* Sometimes this involves actually snapping off the fly but more often an audible crack of the leader. In either case, this whip-cracking effect is caused by:
   a. starting the forward cast while the backcast is still in progress; or

b. making such a weak backcast that it can't straighten before the forward cast begins.

4. *Splashing the fly down too hard:* This is caused by aiming the cast too low or by unintentionally pulling back on the rod tip before the cast is complete. Aim the cast higher, a couple of feet over the water. The line will straighten in the air and then fall to the surface.

5. *Collapse of the forward cast:* This is caused by:
    a. releasing extra line into the cast before completing the power stroke; or
    b. driving the rod tip so far down, the loop is collapsed from the bottom.

Now try to get in some practice in the yard or on the stream. Remember, above all, straight lines and tight loops!

Recommended Books

Fly Casting With Lefty Kreh (J. B. Lippincott Company, 1974). This book is the best one I have seen in illustrating photographically the art of a superb fly caster. Using motor-driven cameras, Herman Kessler and Irv Swope provide sequence photos showing the second-by-second development of the cast. Fly casting at its best.

Fly Fishing Strategy by Doug Swisher and Carl Richards (Crown Publishers, Inc., 1975). This is a more recent book by the pair that produced *Selective Trout*, which will be recommended later. The book is aimed at experienced fly fishermen, but the chapter on casting is particularly helpful.

4
ACCESSORIES:
Selection and Maintenance

Obviously, fly anglers need more than a rod, reel, line, and leader to be successful. They need flies, of course, and a way to carry them. They need special equipment for wading, and they need various gadgets and accessories that will make their time astream more productive and pleasant. Most of all, they need a plan for selecting this equipment and for maintaining it in a good state of repair at a moderate cost.

Like other fishermen, fly anglers carry much equipment with them on their outings. Unlike other fishermen, fly anglers most often fish on foot, and they usually must cover considerable ground. So fly fishermen cannot rely on the tackle box, like boating anglers, and yet they must carry almost as much in the way of lures and gadgets. The dual requirements of preparedness and mobility have led to the development of specialized equipment and techniques, some of them absolutely essential to success and enjoyment, others of no more than passing interest. We'll try to separate the essential from the frivolous.

If you are like most anglers, you will progress through three steps. First, as a beginner, you will often find yourself astream without a needed article of equipment. The frustration will lead you to the second stage, where you will be carrying so much tackle you'll look like a walking fly shop. Finally, as an experienced angler, you will reach stage three, about a third lighter than stage two, where you know from experience exactly what you need and carry only that.

The purpose of this chapter is not to eliminate this process. Each angler personally journeys through these stages, learning all along the way. What I will try to do is tell you something about the equipment and accessories that I have found useful. You will not need all of them all of the time, but selecting from them when planning an excursion will make your outings more profitable and pleasant.

Fly Boxes

Fly boxes could fill an entire chapter by themselves. When you consider the purchase of a fly box, remember that the types of flies that you intend to carry in it is the major consideration. Dry flies require boxes that will not crush the hackles or bend the tails. Streamers and bucktails require boxes with large compartments. Flies require drying after use, so many fly boxes are ventilated to allow air circulation. If you often fish in the wind, you need specially designed boxes to keep your flies from blowing away every time you open the lid.

Weight and cost are also important considerations. You can't catch fish with a fly box, so my inclination is to use boxes that are as light and inexpensive as possible. The money and weight saved can then be devoted to equipment that actually catches fish.

Dry Fly Boxes

A good dry fly box protects the stiff tails and hackle collars that support many dry flies on the surface of the water. Some boxes accomplish this by providing clips or slots into which the flies can be placed, holding them securely in one safe position. Others are divided into compartments for placing several flies. The compartments provide both a way of separating flies into patterns and a means for keeping them all from gathering in a pile when the box is shifted around. Some boxes are metal, some are plastic. Here is a list of the various types available, along with my personal (and by no means universal) evaluations.

CLIP BOXES. Several metal boxes, of both domestic and foreign manufacture, hold dry flies by a system of clips or springs. First of all, be sure that the box holds flies in an upright position rather than on their sides as in a wet fly box.

- *Advantage:* This is a secure system of holding flies, safe from damage in transit and safe from being blown away.
- *Disadvantages:* Many of these boxes are difficult to get flies into and out of. The clips or springs may dull hook points as the flies are

inserted or withdrawn. And these boxes are usually not as light to carry as plastic boxes.

COMPARTMENTED BOXES WITH INDIVIDUAL LIDS. These boxes, made in Britain, are the Rolls-Royce of fly boxes. They have individual compartments in which several flies of a pattern can be carried, and each of the compartments has its own transparent lid, complete with spring-loaded latch. The boxes, constructed of seamless aluminum, come in several sizes and styles. Some have wet fly clips on one side, individual compartments on the other.

- *Advantages:* You have good security for flies, along with especially good wind protection, since only one compartment is opened at a time. And you can separate flies by pattern or size.
- *Disadvantages:* These boxes are complex and cost a lot. One of the larger of these boxes can cost as much as a graphite fly rod. Still, there is gratification in owning something that is beautifully and carefully made. If you take care of one of these boxes, it could last a lifetime.

COMPARTMENTED PLASTIC BOXES. The least expensive way to carry dry flies is in plastic boxes. The less expensive of these boxes (although nothing made from a petroleum base is really cheap these days) are made

Figure 4–1 A selection of dry fly boxes. *Clockwise from the Right:* The Fly File by Scientific Anglers, an English Wheatley box with individual compartments, a light-weight tenite plastic box from Orvis. (Photo by Katherine G. Lee)

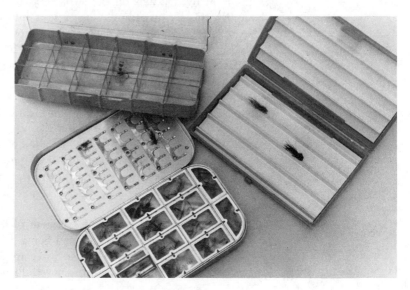

of clear, relatively thick plastic. They are the same boxes used by other hobbyists for separating small objects.

- *Advantages:* These are about the cheapest boxes you can own, and they are available in a wide range of sizes and compartment designs.
- *Disadvantages:* These are heavier than other plastic boxes; they don't last long because their plastic hinges break; and they may react chemically with head cement or fly floatant to make a real mess.

The more expensive plastic boxes are made of a lightweight plastic called Tenite, and they have durable metal hinges. Most of them have colored bottoms (one manufacturer covers the bottoms with a carpet-like material) and clear lids. These boxes float, and they are strong enough to support a man (although they can't do both at the same time). They will not react with chemicals found in head cement, line cleaner, or fly floatant.

- *Advantages:* They are low-cost and extremely light-weight, and they offer good fly protection.
- *Disadvantages:* They offer less wind protection than clip or individually covered compartment boxes.

BOXES WITH MAGNETIC BARS. These boxes feature nonmetallic bars that grip the hooks of the flies by magnetism (they have fine metal particles imbedded in them). They hold dry flies well and protect tails and hackles if selected for the size of flies to be carried. They are especially good for very small dry flies.

- *Advantages:* They offer good wind protection, security, and easy organization.
- *Disadvantages:* Somewhat higher in cost than the plastic boxes, these boxes are slightly heavier to carry, and they have a smaller capacity than other boxes of the same overall size.

BOXES THAT HOLD FLIES WITH FOAM. Boxes that hold flies with plastic foam inserts have been on the market for several years, and they are particularly good for nymphs and wet flies. In the mid-seventies, a dry fly version called the Ripple-Foam box was introduced. The box has raised ridges of plastic foam into which the hooks of dry flies can be inserted, offering good protection for fragile hackles and tails.

- *Advantages:* You get good security at no damage to hook points, easy insertion and withdrawal, and good wind security, all in a light-weight container.

- *Disadvantages:* The box is more expensive than a plastic box, and the foam is subject to wear, although new inserts are available at low cost.

Wet Fly Boxes

These boxes hold any of the submerged flies: wets, nymphs, or streamers. Most of the dry fly boxes already discussed can do double duty with wet flies, but boxes especially designed for wet flies do not lend themselves to carrying dry flies.

CLIP BOXES. The classic wet fly box uses rows of clips that hold the fly by the bend of the hook. The sizes of the clips and the spaces between the rows vary depending on the sizes of the flies to be carried. These boxes are available in relatively inexpensive domestic models or in the saltier British version made by the same firm that turns out the individually lidded compartment boxes.

- *Advantages:* You get security without hook point damage, good organization, and plenty of capacity, especially in boxes with extra "pages" of clips.
- *Disadvantages:* These are costlier than plastic boxes and somewhat heavier. Also, flies are more difficult to insert and withdraw.

Figure 4–2 Alternatives for carrying wet flies, streamers, and nymphs. *Clockwise from the Right:* A sheepskin fleece fly book, a home-modified box with foam strips, a Wheatley wet fly box with index to contents. (Photo by Katherine G. Lee)

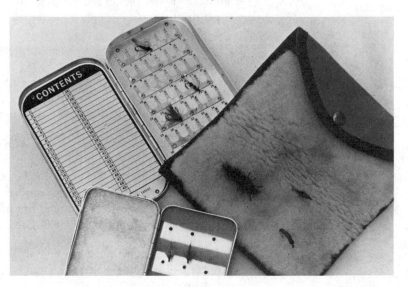

FOAM BOXES. Since wet flies and streamers do not have stiff hackle collars to be protected, flat foam is an ideal medium for storage and transport. Many foam-lined boxes are on the market, and more and more anglers are making their own by modifying other boxes to accept the foam or by cutting foam to fit and gluing it into plastic boxes from other sources. The foam is available at hobby and craft shops.

- *Advantages:* This light-weight box offers good security and lots of capacity for box size.
- *Disadvantages:* There are practically none except that the foam wears out, but replacement foam is readily available.

FLEECE FLY "BOOKS". The fleece book acquired its name because it opens like a book, and some have extra "pages" as well. It holds hooks by shearling fleece, which is usually sewn to a canvas or leather backing. The book is shut with a snap or a zipper.

- *Advantages:* The flies are held securely while being easy to insert and withdraw. You also have large capacity in a small, flat package.
- *Disadvantages:* Flies reinserted immediately after use will rust, because the fleece doesn't allow air to circulate around the hook. Flies used from a fleece book must be thoroughly dried before being placed into the book again.

Leader Materials

In addition to flies, the angler must carry extra leaders and leader materials. Extra leaders are most easily carried in a *leader wallet,* which consists of several clear plastic sleeves with a leather or plastic cover to protect them.

Spools of leader material are carried not to build entire leaders but to replace tippets (the last strand of the leader to which the fly is attached) or to rebuild the taper section (more about that in Chapter 5). While the exact sizes of material needed vary with the fish being sought, material from 2X to 7X is commonly needed in freshwater fly fishing. Some vests have small pockets just for leader spools. Some anglers run a string through the holes of the spools and carry them all together that way. A gadget, called a "leader dispenser," contains six small spools inside a round plastic housing. Each spool feeds out a strand of material through a hole in the housing; the monofilament can be pulled out and then cut to the desired length on a little cutter provided for each spool.

Here is a list of gadgets you might consider using, divided according to my views into what's essential and nonessential paraphernalia. Needless to say, keep in mind that what's essential and what isn't is a matter of opinion. So consult other anglers if you have questions.

Essential

1. *Nail clippers*. These are used to clip leader material after tying on a fly or tying a leader knot. They are used literally hundreds, maybe thousands, of times during the fishing season. The cheapest kind you can find will do well if you change them every year as they get dull. The fancier kind sold in fly shops should last longer and stay sharper, and they usually feature other built-in gizmos, such as knife blades or needle points for poking head cement out of the eye of a fly.

2. *Hemostats*. Also called forceps, these are used by surgeons to clamp off blood vessels during operations. They make great hook disgorgers since they lock in a clamped position. They can also be used as a temporary vise for streamside fly tying, and the smooth area back of the serrated jaws can be used to bend the barbs down on large flies if you don't carry anything else. Hemostats come straight or curved in several sizes. Most anglers prefer the medium-sized curved ones. Get your doctor to give you a pair or, if he can't afford that, buy them from your local medical supply store.

3. *Stream thermometer*. Water temperature, a critical variable in the behavior of both fish and aquatic insects, is a piece of information that you should have. Get the kind of thermometer that stream biologists use, and use it often. The best ones have a pen clip and also a ring on the tip to attach a line to for extra security.

4. *Fly floatant*. Most anglers like to dab a little fly floatant on their dry flies before casting them. The flies float better, especially in rough water, because they do not absorb moisture so rapidly. Several types are on the market: spray, liquid, and paste. The spray types are wasteful and bulky to carry. I like the paste type best, but many of my fishing friends use the liquid. If it gets hot enough, the paste turns to liquid anyway, so I'm covered.

5. *Sunglasses*. Sunglasses serve two purposes for the angler. First, of course, they cut glare and minimize eyestrain. More importantly, good sunglasses allow the angler to see into the water to spot fish

54

that would otherwise be invisible. For both these purposes the glasses you choose must be "polarized." Polarizing is a process that screens light coming to the eye at an angle. Since most glare in fishing situations results from light reflected from the water's surface, polarized lenses are far superior to any others for fishing.

If you wear glasses already, you may wish to order prescription sunglasses with polarized lenses. If you do not need prescription glasses, or if you buy clip-on glasses to fit over your present eyeglasses, you will have a wider choice of lens colors. I prefer the light grey lenses under most conditions, and they are the best on shady trout streams. For river fishing, where the glare is much greater, I like the green lenses. Many anglers favor brown because it cuts glare well while preserving contrasts.

6. *Hook hone.* More strikes are lost to dull hooks than to any other factor. You should be prepared to sharpen hooks on the stream, and this will be especially necessary when fishing bottom-bouncing flies like streamers and nymphs. Of the many types and sizes of hook hones available, the small ones are best for freshwater fly fishing. You can sharpen a large hook with a small hone, but the opposite is not true. For extremely small hooks, pointed sharpening stones may be necessary. These can be ordered through angling catalogs if you need them.

7. *Lead.* Unpleasant though it may be to cast, it is often necessary to weight the leader to get the fly down to where the fish are. Split shot or lead wire is most often used for this purpose. I like the split shot that comes in a round plastic pack divided into four sections for different-sized shot. For weighting larger or more buoyant flies, the larger removable split shot are good. They have little ears on the side opposite the split, so they can be opened and removed without clipping off the fly. This feature makes them reusable too.

Lead in split-tube design has become available in sizes small enough to be used by the fly rodder. Advocates say that the tube design offers less air resistance to the cast than the bulkier shot. I don't know about that. I do know that the split tube lead that I bought was far more expensive than shot, far more difficult to get out of the package (since the tubes only roll in two directions, they bind up under the swiveling lid), and more prone to come off the leader in casting. I prefer the split shot.

8. *Insect repellent.* Not all bugs are as friendly as the ones that our flies imitate. The active ingredient in bug dope is N-Diethyl-meta-toluamide. The higher the percentage of N-Diethyl-whatever, the more effective the repellent will be. Most anglers I know carry not only a spray can in the car for dousing themselves before they start fishing, but also a small stick or squeeze bottle for supplementing later on.

9. *Emergency kit.* At least for prolonged excursions you should have a small package of emergency supplies. I like to carry a small first aid kit, some aspirin, a snake-bite kit, a few antiseptic towelettes, some toilet paper, and a folding drinking cup. All this goes into a plastic box, and then the box goes into an air-tight plastic bag. Waterproof, the package can be kept out of the way until needed.

10. *Knife.* A knife has a thousand uses, on the stream and off. I favor the small version of the Swiss Army Knife because it contains not only blades but scissors, file, and a number of other useful tools.

Nonessential (But Often Nice to Have)

1. *Insect collecting equipment.* Collecting specimens of available insects can sometimes mean the difference between success and failure. Flying insects can be caught in your hand or in your hat, but a small net that attaches to your rod tip is a lot better. A nymph net that rolls up in your pocket is useful for capturing immature insects. A dime store aquarium net is a great help in plucking insects off the surface (an almost impossible task with your bare hand). The twisted wire handle can be bent to fit your pocket or to slip over your belt. Add a couple of small collecting jars for taking samples home, and you are prepared for insect collecting.

2. *Reverse-acting tweezers.* Although these have become essentials for me, other anglers get along without them, so I've put them on the nonessential list. These tweezers, which open when squeezed and shut when released, allow me to pick up tiny flies with ease. Poking around in a midge box with my big fingers would make a real mess. Once the fly is selected, I use the tweezers for holding it while I tie it on the tippet. These are highly recommended.

3. *Sinking solution.* You need floatant to float dry flies, and you may also need a sinking agent to get the wet ones under quickly. This material works by speeding up the capillary action by which materials become saturated. If you think that sinking your leader while fishing dry flies is important, the solution will work on that as well as wet flies, nymphs, and streamers. Saliva also works well as a sink agent; at least it allows saturating the fly before casting it. The great Ray Bergman used to soak his nymphs in his mouth before fishing them. If you don't want to go that far, buy some sink agent.

4. *Fly drying granules.* These are small silicone granules, about the size of table sugar, that will dry a sopping fly so that it will float again.

They are especially good for refloating a dry fly after a fish has been caught with it. You drop the fly in a tube of the granules, with the leader still attached. Then cover the tube with your hand and shake it. The fly collects granules and comes out looking like a heavily salted ham. The granules pull the moisture and fish slime out of the fly. After a minute you blow off most of the granules, false cast off the rest, re-treat the fly with your regular floatant, and start fishing again. Ordinarily, it's better and less trouble just to change to a fresh fly. But when you have only a couple of the pattern the fish are taking, this material can be a lifesaver.

5. *Leader straightener*. Leader material tends to take on the shape of the coil it has been stored in, and it must be straightened before fishing. You can do this between your thumb and forefinger; in fact that's the best way once you get a good callous developed. Until then, a piece of old inner tube will do the job, as long as you don't squeeze so hard that you scorch and weaken the leader. My personal preference is for a piece of pigskin, cut from an old shoe. It seems to straighten the leader easily without building up excessive heat.

6. *Needle-nose pliers*. These are used to flatten barbs on hooks. They should be light-weight and have smooth jaws. Most pliers have serrated jaws, and the hook barb slides into the grooves and remains intact. Even better than needle-nose pliers, if you can get them, are the dental pliers used in orthodontic work. These have narrow little jaws, smooth and flat. Lacking either of these, you can use the smooth part of your hemostats, but small flies will be a problem unless you carry something specifically for de-barbing them.

7. *Fly threader*. If you have trouble with your eyesight, one of these little tools might be helpful. There's a little cone on top; you put the hook eye in one end and thread the leader tippet through the other. Pull the tippet out of the slot, and the fly is on . . . most of the time.

8. *Jeweler's loupe*. If you have trouble seeing, this may be the best solution to the problem. It is a small magnifying lens that fits over your eyeglass frames, swinging up out of the way when not needed and flipping down to magnify when necessary. These can be ordered through fly fishing catalogs or through jewelers. One caution is don't order high power: 2 or 3X is plenty, even for tying on size 24 and 26 flies. Any higher power reduces the depth of field and requires holding the fly and leader closer to the eye than is comfortable.

9. *Lights*. Evening or early morning fishing often call for some sort of illumination. One solution is the Flex-Light, which clips to a pocket like a pen and has a flexible neck to swivel in all directions.

Another is the Lens-Lite, which hangs around the neck on a cord and features a magnifying lens as well as a light. Finally, there is the Bite-Lite, a tiny bulb with a battery inside a flexible plastic housing that, when squeezed, illuminates the bulb. It can be held in the mouth and bitten down on to light the working area.

In addition to these lights for tying on flies and other actual fishing purposes, most anglers carry a small flashlight for lighting their way back to the car after the evening hatch. Disposable flashlights are favored because they are small and light. Remember to dispose of them properly.

10. *Knot tiers*. Although my bias is that a fly fisherman ought to be able to tie the basic knots without aid (and probably blindfolded), some anglers find knot tiers very helpful. These gadgets are tools for tying every knot imaginable, and some unimaginable ones too. Consult your catalog.

11. *Leader gauge*. Leader gauges measure the diameter of nylon monofilament in thousandths of an inch. Micrometers used to be required for such precision, but they were heavy and expensive. The newer gauges do the same job, without a heavy weight and cost penalty.

12. *Fly line cleaner*. The tip of a floating fly line gradually sinks under the surface as it collects dirt and algae. Fly line cleaner cleans and refloats the line in no time. A small tin of fly line cleaner is no trouble to tuck into your vest or fishing shirt. If you find it more convenient, line cleaner is also available in moist towelette form.

13. *Stomach pump*. The stomach pump allows the angler to examine what the fish has been eating without conducting an autopsy. It is a simple plastic tube with a squeeze bulb on one end, usually with a pen clip for attaching to a pocket. In use, the bulb is used to fill the tube partially with water. The tube is then inserted down the fish's throat into the gullet, the water is squirted in and then drawn out again. With it comes the most recent meal, along with some half-digested bits of earlier repasts.

It takes practice to use the pump easily and safely, but it can give the angler highly important information at little harm to the fish. If you are a hatch-matching fisherman (and you'll find out later if you are), this might be a good accessory for you. One caution: You'll find that some of your friends and family may have been harboring the idea that fly fishermen are crazy. When they find you have purchased this little item, they will no longer have any doubt.

14. *Landing net*. Many anglers prefer not to use a landing net because they intend to release the fish anyway and don't really care if one escapes while being played or landed. On the other hand, a landing

net can be a real advantage to an angler who releases fish, since you can handle a fish in the net and remove the hook with less chance of injury.

15. *Creel.* Those who want to take some fish home for eating need something for storage and transporting the catch. The old basket style creel of split willow construction is one possibility, while the new creels work by the principle of cooling by water evaporation. Either way, a creel takes up a lot of room and seems to be in the way most of the time.

16. *Priest.* This is a club for dispatching fish that are to be taken home. I suppose the name derives from the fact that they are used to deliver the "last rites." Despite their title, priests are faintly distasteful to many anglers in this day of catch-and-release fishing, and they are no longer as heavily advertised as they once were. Still, if a fish is to be kept, a merciful and quick death with a club is far preferable to slow expiration in a creel or on a stringer.

17. *Tape measure.* For anglers who like to know the exact size of their catch, a tape measure can be desirable. It is certainly preferable to scales, which may injure fish that are going to be released. My own preference is to make a mark on the rod at a known distance from the handle; fish length can be "eye-balled" from there. Whatever the method, you can reliably estimate the weight of a fish if you know the length.

18. *Rain gear.* On most fishing trips, at least a rain jacket is desirable. This can be the top half of an inexpensive rain suit, available at most discount and hardware stores. Wading anglers do not need the pants, but they may be needed when fishing from a boat. The cheap suits have very little air circulation, so they can be miserably uncomfortable if worn for a long period. If you like to fish in the rain (and that can be an excellent time to be on the water), one of the better rain jackets with good ventilation would be well worth the expense.

19. *Scissors.* Scissors are useful for trimming hackle on flies, cutting leader material, or reshaping a fly to more closely resemble a natural insect. One type of scissors features flat tips for squeezing split shot tightly onto the leader. The small folding scissors available in most fabric stores are favored by some anglers.

20. *Hat.* Some sort of hat with a brim is desirable, both for shading the eyes and for minimizing the bother of insects. Many small insects, particularly gnats, will drive you crazy buzzing around your eyes, and insect repellent seems to have no effect on them. These same insects, however, will not go into the shade, so if you wear something that throws your eyes into shade you will not be bothered. If a regular hat is too hot, the topless brims worn by golfers do just as well.

As these lists make clear, fly anglers need to carry a lot of equipment in as painless a manner as possible. For most anglers, that method is the fly fishing vest: a sleeveless garment, loaded with pockets and organized as a coherent storage and transportation system.

The fishing vest was invented and sewn together by master angler Lee Wulff back in the 1930s. Since then many companies have designed and manufactured vests in all price ranges and levels of quality. If you stick with fly fishing, sooner or later you will buy a vest, perhaps several of them. The best vests usually have most or all of the following features:

High-Quality Material
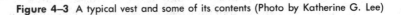

These days "high quality" usually means a blend of cotton and polyester. The material should be strong and quick drying.

Double Stitching

Vests can get pretty heavy when stuffed full of all the gear a fly angler carries. The seams that carry the load, around the shoulders and neck and the pockets, should be double stitched.

Figure 4–3 A typical vest and some of its contents (Photo by Katherine G. Lee)

Lots of Pockets

Good vests not only have an adequate number of pockets but pockets of different sizes, designed to accommodate standard-sized fly boxes. The large pockets should be of the "bellows" design, which allows the pocket to expand outward to accept an extra box or additional gadget without tearing. Good quality vests also have special pockets designed for sunglasses, leader wallets, and spools of leader material.

Velcro and Zipper Closing

Avoid vests with snap closings. You can't shut the pockets with one hand. They will drive you crazy. Velcro is desirable as closing material for pockets that don't carry a great deal of weight. All you need to do is slap the pocket flap down, and it is securely shut. Zippers, required on big pockets and on those that are opened only occasionally, should be of the vinyl, self-healing type, with big pull tabs for easy grabbing. Nothing on the vest should be subject to rust.

Storage for Seldom Needed Items

Most vests have a large pocket across the back for carrying emergency gear, lunch, and other seldom needed items. In most cases, the vest has to be taken off to get things out of this pocket, so don't plan to store things there that you need regularly.

Attachment Gear

A vest should have some built-in gear for attaching nets, creels, and other accessories. Usually there are a couple of D-rings on the vest for this purpose. Pin-on fleece patches are very desirable, too. They are used to park used flies (finish drying them out when you get home), so you don't have to put each one back in its box before tying on another. The pin-on feature makes it possible to move the patch to a convenient location or to remove it altogether if necessary.

Vest Accessories

Although accessories don't come with the vest, they are worth considering as additions when you purchase your vest. Most important in this category are the small pin-on retracting reels to which you can attach frequently used items, such as your clippers. You pull the item down for use and the retractor reels it back up out of the way when you're finished. I've heard some anglers question the reliability of these little retractors, but I have had four on my vest for seven years without a single
61 failure. You might also consider the larger retracting reels that are sold

in most hardware stores. These are designed for carrying large rings of keys but they can be just the ticket for keeping bulky items, like landing nets, out of the way until needed.

The final vest accessory is inexpensive but valuable: safety pins. They can be used to make too-small zipper tabs easy to grab. They can poke head cement out of the eye of a fly. They can mend a rip in your clothes. They can even be used to fashion a temporary rod guide if you need one in an emergency. Pin several to the inside of your vest.

Size

A final consideration in the selection of a fishing vest is size. You will probably find it desirable to get your vest large enough so that you can wear a jacket under it comfortably. Length is important too. If you fish a lot in water where you wade deep, a "shorty" vest, designed to be worn with chest waders, might suit your needs. You give up some capacity with a shorty, but you can wade to the tops of your waders and still keep your equipment dry.

Organization

Whatever the features of the vest you choose, you will find yourself arranging and rearranging your gear until everything is comfortable and just where you want it. Ultimately, you want a storage system that you know so well that you can reach for what you want without thinking and come up with it on the first try.

I've found it useful to organize my own vest by fly categories. My standard dry flies are in the left front pocket. My caddis patterns and terrestrials are in the right front. Nymphs and wets are on the inside left, and streamers on the inside right. Small inside pockets hold leader material, arranged according to diameter, and other small items like split shot, lead wire, and line cleaner. The upper left pocket holds my midge imitations in a box with magnetic strips. Next to that is a pocket with my stream thermometer, insect repellent, and fly floatant. The inside left pocket holds my sunglasses. The two pockets on the upper right front hold tiny nymphs and a box of miscellaneous flies, respectively, and behind them, on the inside, is my leader wallet.

Stuffed into some of these pockets, too, are small items like my aquarium net, insect identification booklet, nymph net, eyeglass loupe, and leader sink material. In back is the emergency kit, wader repair kit, rain jacket, and sometimes lunch.

My friend Bob Abraham calls his vest "my tackle box on my back." The best vest is one that you can use in exactly this way. Remember, your purpose is to catch fish, and to catch fish you must be fishing, not fumbling with equipment or rummaging through pockets. Select your vest with care and organize it well. If you do, you will be able to forget it and concentrate on the fishing.

Alternatives to the Vest

Instead of "alternatives," I should say "additions" to the vest, because most fly rodders who use the equipment I'm going to describe already own vests and use them regularly. Yet in some fishing situations the vest is either not needed or a nuisance for one reason or another. If you find yourself in such special circumstances, consider these options:

THE FISHING JACKET. This is basically a simplified vest with sleeves. It may be needed for those in-between times when a vest over a heavy shirt or jacket is too hot but when a vest with a short-sleeved shirt is not warm enough. In a light-weight version, this shirt may be just the thing for fishing in the black fly or mosquito season.

THE CHEST PACK. Sometimes called the Handy Andy, this consists of two packs connected by straps, so that one pack hangs on the chest, the other down the back. The two packs can be easily exchanged in position so that material in the back pack can be reached. The Handy Andy has a couple of advantages: First, it rides higher on the body than most vests, so anglers can wade deeper without getting their equipment wet. Second, the pack suspends the weight from the shoulders instead of from the

Figure 4-4 The chest-and-backpack alternative to the vest. The round item of the upper right is a leader material dispenser. (Photo by Katherine G. Lee)

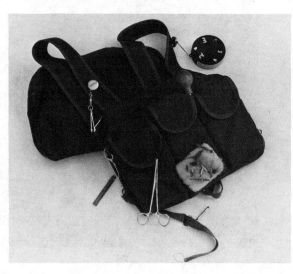

neck, so many fishermen find the Handy Andy more comfortable to wear for extended periods than many vests.

The simplest version of this dual pack arrangement has two basic packs into which a lot of gear can be stuffed. More sophisticated versions have compartments inside, fly box pockets outside, and D-rings for hanging on more accessories.

THE CHEST FLY BOX. In much of the country, late summer angling is no picnic in a standard fishing vest due to the heat. One solution, of course, is to invest in a second vest of light-weight mesh material; several are available for hot-weather fishing. Another solution is the chest fly box. This is an aluminum box with several trays that rests against the angler's chest, attached by straps that go over the shoulders. The trays open outwards, and they feature aluminum lids to keep the flies inside from blowing away. In most models, the trays have compartments for dry flies, while the lids feature foam lining for parking wets and nymphs. Additional small items can be stowed in one of the trays or hung from the straps with retracting reels. While the capacity of the chest box is limited in comparison to a vest, it can carry a lot of flies, and its small size and light weight are really appreciated on a hot day.

One drawback to some of these boxes is that their bright aluminum panels may reflect sunlight like a mirror and alarm fish. Some of the boxes are anodized black or green to deal with this problem. If the one you like isn't, you may cut the glare by applying ordinary contact paper to the large panels of the box.

Figure 4–5 A chest fly box. This one was made by J. R. Sadler, The Angler's Box and Tool Company, Springfield, Pa. (Photo by Katherine G. Lee)

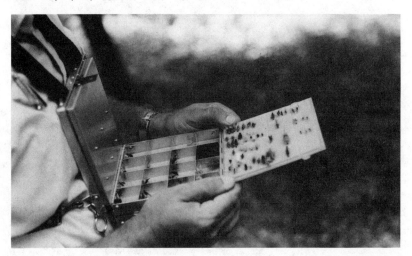

Of all the equipment required for fly fishing, nothing is the cause of more frustration to the average angler than wading equipment. We want and need qualities in wading gear that can't yet be found in a single product: reliability, long life, economy, comfort, and protection from leaks. To get even a few of these features you must generally sacrifice some of the others. Let's examine the options in wading gear, and then look at the advantages and disadvantages of each.

Hip Boots

These "hippers" are either rubber or a combination of rubber and fabric and reach to the hips of a wading angler. They are most suited for small stream fishing, but most anglers own a pair even if they also have the larger chest waders, simply because hippers are more comfortable and are handy to use if the length is adequate.

Most hip boots have an inside fastening arrangement that snaps around the upper calf and loops that go around the belt to hold them up. The problem is that the weight of the boots pulls your pants down. To compensate for this tendency, some anglers buy a hip boot "harness," which suspends the boots from the shoulders instead of from the belt. I have no experience with the harness, but I do have lots of experience in pulling my pants up, so I suspect it is a good idea.

Most essential in a hip boot, or in a chest wader for that matter, is reliable footing. The deep lug soles found on so many inexpensive hip boots are adequate only for streams with mud bottoms. Rocky streams, in which many gamefish are found, require soles with much greater traction. The favored material today is felt or woven polyester material which, when glued to the soles of the boots, grips slippery rocks with much greater tenacity than rubber. Some very expensive hip boots have metal studs in addition to felt on the soles. The metal spikes that protrude through the sole add greatly to the gripping power.

Naturally, felt soles wear out fairly rapidly, especially when the angler walks on dry ground or roads in addition to the stream bottom. Kits are available for replacing felt soles, and many anglers replace soles several times in the life of a pair of hip boots. These kits can also be used to add felt soles to rubber-soled hip boots.

Hip boots range in price from inexpensive, such as those in your local discount store, to very expensive, such as those in some catalogs and fly shops. Although the expensive hip boots are probably better than the cheap ones, there are so many exceptions to this rule that spending a lot of money for hip boots does not really guarantee freedom from problems. A friend of mine bought a cheap pair of imported hip boots ten years ago and glued some carpet to the soles. He is still using them today. I know another fellow who paid about seventy dollars for a pair ordered from a catalog, only to get soaked the first time he stepped into the stream.

My own solution to the hip boot problem, so far at least, has been to buy rubber-soled boots in the low to medium price range and add felt soles to them myself. With proper care (more to come on that topic), my boots have lasted three to four seasons; and, from what I hear from other anglers, that's a little better than average.

Chest Waders

As the name indicates, chest waders allow much deeper wading than hip boots. For that reason, well prepared anglers need a pair in most parts of the country. As a rule, waders cost more than hip boots, and they are usually worn under conditions where malfunction can mean inconvenience, discomfort, or even real danger. So many anglers are willing to spend more for high-quality waders than for hippers. Like hip boots, however, a high price is no guarantee of quality, although most of the major manufacturers assure your satisfaction if something goes wrong early in the life of the product.

In addition to decisions about price range and quality, anglers considering the purchase of chest waders must also decide on which foot style best suits their needs. Waders are available either in *boot foot* models, with feet like the hip boots complete with either rubber or felt soles, or in *stocking foot* models, which require the addition of a wading shoe. The stocking foot models are usually more comfortable and trouble-free, especially for a long day of fishing, because the wading shoe provides better support, and usually better traction, than the boot foot model can offer. The disadvantages are their higher cost (since separate wading shoes must be purchased) and more trouble getting ready to fish (a pair of heavy socks next to the skin, then the waders, then another pair of socks, then the wading shoes).

Fly anglers who use waders a lot usually prefer the stocking foot models. For those for whom deep wading is only an occasional requirement, the less expensive and less complicated boot foot version is probably best. Again, felt soles are recommended, whatever the style of wader chosen.

Wet Wading

Wet wading, of course, is wading with no equipment other than perhaps special shoes. In the hot months wet wading can be a sheer delight, a combination of fishing and swimming at the same time. Traction, however, remains an important consideration. Getting injured by falling in the low-water streams of late summer is probably easier than doing so in the heavier flows of the early season. For this reason, many anglers who wet wade regularly wear the same high-quality wading shoes as those used by the wearers of stocking foot waders. These shoes not only provide good traction, but they also protect the upper foot and ankle from stone bruises and decrease the likelihood of sprained ankles.

Those who wet wade less frequently can often get by with tennis shoes, but the slippery combination of water and rubber makes them dangerous unless you do something to improve traction. To add traction to tennis shoes, get some scraps of indoor-outdoor carpet, cut them to fit the outline of the soles, and take them to your local shoe shop. Ask the shoemaker to glue the carpet to the soles and put the shoes in the shoe press overnight. You will get a funny look, even after you explain your purpose, but the carpet will be there for a long time. The price is right too. My shoe shop charges me four dollars for this work, and the shoes I use are tennis shoes already worn beyond use on the tennis court. The traction is every bit as good as my felt-soled hippers, and maybe better.

Wading Accessories

You might find a number of specialized items useful in making your wading safer and more comfortable. Here are a couple you can look for:

Figure 4–6 Three approaches to the wading shoe. *Clockwise from the Lower Right:* The traditional shoe—leather, canvas, and piano-felt soles, from the Russell Moccasin Company; the innovative shoe—waterproof suede, plastic mesh, and poly-felt soles, from the Danner Shoe Company; and the cheap shoe—old sneakers with carpet glued to the soles. (Photo by Katherine G. Lee)

WADING SANDALS OR CHAINS. These fit either over the foot of a boot foot wader or hipper or over a wading shoe to provide super traction on extremely slick surfaces. In a fast-flowing river with a slippery bottom, they may be an absolute necessity for safe wading. They can be removed and carried when not needed.

WADING STAFF. This staff adds to the wader's protection by providing support when braced against the stream bottom. One fairly expensive version folds up into a small package until needed, then springs out and snaps together when taken out of the little pack it is carried in.

If you use a noncollapsible wading staff, a heavy-duty chain reel retractor may help keep it handy and yet out of the way. With the retractor snapped to the belt, the staff trails in the current behind you until needed. Consider also making your own wading staff or adapting some other stick for the purpose. I have angling friends who have cut and carved their own staffs, not to mention someone who made one from aluminum tubing. My wading staff was once a ski pole.

While these accessories can make your wading more comfortable, nothing can make it more fun until technology comes to the aid of the wading angler. The years have seen some improvements, but water-proof pants are still generally uncomfortable, unreliable, and expensive. Fly anglers complain constantly about wading gear, but as yet no one has done anything substantial to improve the situation.

Equipment Maintenance

As the preceding portion of this chapter shows, fly fishing equipment can represent a considerable financial expenditure. So maintaining and caring for your equipment properly are important to insure long life and reliable service. Here are some quick suggestions for the proper storage and maintenance of your valuable equipment:

Rods

Rods should be thoroughly dried after each outing and returned to their rod bags and protective tubes. If you don't have these protective items, you can easily make them. Bags can be made from any rot-proof cloth, following a factory rod bag as a model. Tubes can be made from PVC plumbing pipe available at your local hardware store. Fittings can also be purchased to make threaded caps for each end. You can drill small holes in each of the caps for ventilation.

Rods should not be kept set up for extended periods. Bamboo rods especially should receive faithful care and careful storage. They should be stored in a dry, moderately warm area, and it's best to store them so the sections are vertical.

Reels

Reels usually do not require special care during the fishing season, other than an occasional lubrication with a light water-proof grease such as Lubriplate. If reels are used in salt water, however, they should be thoroughly rinsed in fresh water immediately, along with the rods and any other equipment subject to corrosion. For off-season storage, lines should be removed from reels. The reels themselves should be washed in warm water and soap, dried by hand, air dried, and then lightly lubricated. Reel bags are good places for storage, once the reels are dry. Reel bags can also be home-made if your reels did not come with them.

Fly Lines

Lines store best off the reels, so that they do not take a tight kink from being stored in small coils. Fancy line winders are available for line storage, but I have found that #10 tin cans, like those that fruit juices come in, are ideal for line storage. Remove the label and cut out both ends of the can with a can opener. Wind on the line (leader first, if you have chosen to leave it on) along the reinforcing ribs of the can; each can holds three lines comfortably. Secure the last wrap of the line to the can with a piece of masking tape, and use a stick-on label under each line to identify the size and taper. When the fishing season comes around again, just have a friend hold the can while you wind the line directly back onto the reel.

It's a good idea to clean your lines before storing them. Since they should be kept out of strong light, a dark closet is best for prolonged storage.

Flies

Flies must be stored carefully, because they are subject to both rust and moth damage. Make sure that no soaked flies are in your boxes; one damp fly can rust all the rest. Store flies in a dry place with a few moth flakes or crystals for protection. Misshapen or bedraggled flies can be restored to their original shape by holding them in the steam from a boiling tea kettle for a few seconds.

Fly Boxes

Before winter, I like to empty the flies out of my boxes and clean them a little if needed. This is a good time to cull flies that are too damaged to be used in the coming season or those that need a steam session to be rejuvenated. If you use the clear plastic fly boxes, check to make sure that no rubber or latex flies remain in them over the storage period.

Leader Material

This material requires no special care except that, like fly lines, it should be kept from direct light as much as possible.

Vests and Clothing

Storage time is a good time to wash and repair vests, packs, and other clothing and accessories. While you are doing so, you can check the various odds and ends carried in the vest for wear and damage, making notes for repair or replacement as necessary.

Wading Gear

Proper care and maintenance are critical with wading equipment. It is subject to rot (especially from the inside), mildew, and chemical deterioration from the interaction of the rubber with ozone in the air and with solvents that may be in the storage area.

Boots and waders should be dried as soon as possible after use, with special attention to the inside of the boots since perspiration can make them as wet inside as they get outside. Boots and waders should be hung by the feet on special boot hangers to allow air to circulate inside. Even better, if possible, is drying the inside of the boots with a hair dryer or the family vacuum cleaner with the control set on reverse. For the ultimate in boot protection, special boot dryers rapidly dry the boots from the inside. If you use expensive waders a lot, these dryers might be a worthwhile investment.

Boots and waders should be stored in the dark during the off-season. Some manufacturers recommend hanging their waders from special boot hangers during the off-season, while others recommend folding the waders and packing them in the original box. There is controversy about which method is best, but you should probably follow the directions that came with your equipment so that you can present a good case should your boots deteriorate over the off-season. Many anglers store their rubber wading gear in plastic garbage bags. These bags keep out light and chemicals that might cause deterioration. Never store boots in your car trunk; the gasoline fumes will shorten their life drastically.

Storage time is a good time to assess the condition of wading gear, making notes to order new felt soles, socks, or other accessories. All too often, you'll find it necessary to order new waders or hippers too.

Most of this care and maintenance takes only a few minutes, but it pays big dividends in increased service and pleasure from your equipment. And it can also become one of the pleasant rituals of fly fishing. Many a cold winter's night has been warmed just a bit by tying flies, lubricating reels, or building new leaders for the coming fishing season. A howling wind, a crackling fire, and a box of flies to sort can combine to conjure up a pleasant fantasy of spring and rising fish. And if anyone should accuse you of "playing with your tackle," you can recite all the advantages of proper maintenance!

5
BETWEEN THE LINE AND THE FLY
Knots and Leaders

I was waist deep in the river. It had been a poor summer for smallmouth bass fishing. Heavy rains had kept the river high and cloudy, and this August evening was only my second attempt to fish under reasonably favorable conditions. So far, I was disappointed. The fishing had been only fair, and I had landed and released several small bass. I was changing flies often, trying to find the pattern that would interest the larger bass.

As I clipped off the last of my tippet, I realized that I had no monofilament of the proper diameter to replace it. After a futile search through my vest, I attached a new tippet several thousandths of an inch smaller than the original. I knew as I tied it that the blood knot was not a reliable connection between two pieces of nylon that differed by more than two or three thousandths of an inch, and yet I could not remember how to tie the surgeon's knot, which I knew was the proper connection under these circumstances. I made a mental note to look up the surgeon's knot later in the evening and tied the brown marabou muddler to the tippet.

As luck would have it, the first cast betrayed the inadequacy of my knot. As the big streamer swept by a boulder, it was intercepted savagely—and the knot exploded as the bass turned away with the fly. All this activity took place in only a few inches of water, so I could both see and hear the failure of my terminal tackle. Even worse, even though the streamer was no longer attached to the leader, the fish was securely hooked. The bass jumped four times in clear view, with the muddler still dangling from the corner of its jaw. It was about eighteen inches long and probably better than three pounds.

It was the best fish I saw that summer. . . .

Fly fishermen lose a lot of good fish due to poorly tied or improper knots. When you consider that eight or ten knots may be tied in an average tapered leader, along with a knot connecting the leader to the line and another tying the fly to the tippet, you have a dozen points of potential trouble. Nevertheless, most failures happen, as in my case, because anglers fail to learn all the knots that are needed or because they fail to tie them carefully and well.

This chapter includes five basic knots, with an additional variation on one of them. You may someday wish to know and use other knots, and sources at the end of the chapter will expand your knotting know-how. The ones presented here, however, are basic, and with them you can meet most freshwater fly fishing situations. I urge you to practice these five knots until you can tie them in your sleep. A reliable knot is one tied by a relaxed, confident angler. Don't wait until the poor light of late evening, when you're surrounded by rising fish, to start learning the knot you need.

Here are the essential knots, with illustrations. I'll suggest the proper conditions under which to use them, and I'll offer a few opinions on the merits and shortcomings of each.

Turle Knot

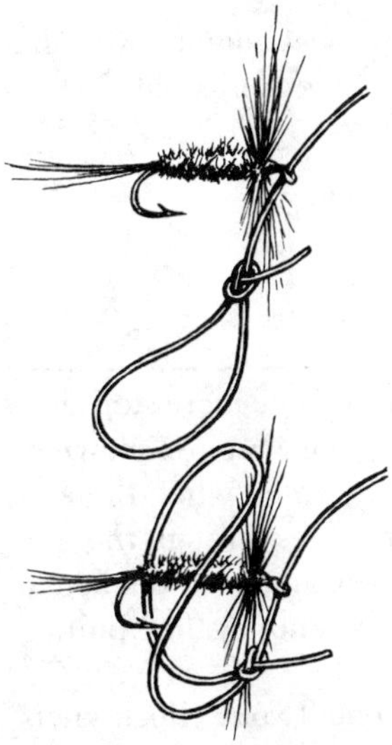

Figure 5–1
The turle knot. The line is intentionally enlarged to show detail.

This knot is used to fasten the fly to the tippet. As you can see from Figure 5–1, you first thread the fly onto the leader tippet and then form a knot that is ultimately drawn over the fly and secured to the head of the fly, right behind the hook eye. The turle knot is actually tied on the fly itself, and herein lies both its advantages and disadvantages.

- *Advantages:* The turle knot provides an absolutely straight line of pull due to the perfect alignment between the leader and the hook shank.
- *Disadvantages:* The turle knot is not as easy to tie as some others, and it is not very strong. It requires somewhat more tippet length to complete, which means you have to extend your tippet sooner than you might if using some other knot. Most importantly, the turle knot leaves a knot still on the fly after the fly has been clipped from the leader. This is the greatest disadvantage of the turle knot. I have sometimes picked the head of a fly apart while trying to dislodge a turle knot with a needle. More often, I have forgotten the knot altogether until I'm ready to use the fly again; so I not only have to tie a new knot, but first of all I have to get rid of the old one.

Nevertheless, in some situations the perfectly straight pull of the turle knot is desirable. I sometimes use the turle knot when fishing with midge flies. Since the tiny hooks of these flies have so little gap, a slight deviation in pull in setting the hook will miss the fish altogether. The turle knot's perfect alignment with the leader can reduce the number of missed strikes under these conditions.

Clinch Knot

Figure 5–2
The clinch knot

This is the simplest and quickest of the fly-to-tippet knots. As Figure 5–2 shows, the clinch knot is made by passing the tippet through the eye of the hook, wrapping the short end around the standing portion several times, sliding the end back through the opening formed by the first wrap-around, and then pulling the turns down snug onto the captured end strand. It's a snap to tie, and, if you've done any fishing before, you probably know the clinch knot already. It is a favorite for fastening spinners, snap swivels, sinkers, and such to fishing line.

Tests conducted by a major line manufacturing company indicate that the strength of the clinch knot is a function of the number of turns made around the standing portion of the leader. Five full turns are recommended.

- *Advantages:* The clinch is simple to tie and strong when properly tied. It clips cleanly, leaving no waste on the fly and no curl in the tippet.
- *Disadvantages:* It does not provide the perfect alignment of the turle knot; while it rarely breaks, it sometimes pulls out.

Improved Clinch Knot

Figure 5–3
The improved clinch knot

In the improved clinch, the end of the tippet is taken one more step after being passed through the loop formed by the original wrap. As shown in Figure 5–3, the end is passed through the loop formed when the end piece is taken from its final wrap up the standing line, through the first wrap opening. Although this addition doesn't add much to the actual breaking strength of the knot, it does protect the knot against pulling out.

If you want this additional protection, then all your clinch knots should be improved. At the very least, you should use the improved clinch when fishing streamers or other flies that are fished with motion.

If a fish strikes while you're manipulating the fly, the stress may be too much and too sudden for the standard clinch knot.

Most fly anglers find these two versions of the clinch knot adequate for most fishing situations they encounter. Some other knots are better for fastening on the fly under special circumstances, but they are all more complicated or wasteful of material. After you learn the clinch knots, you'll probably use them most of the time.

Blood Knot

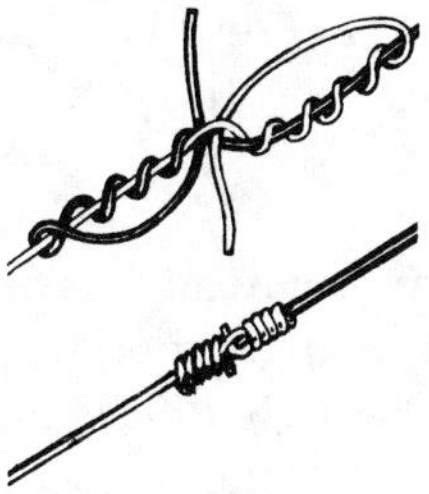

Figure 5–4
The blood knot

The blood knot is the standard knot for joining two strands of leader material, for lengthening your leader when needed, and for adding new tippets as required. As Figure 5–4 shows, the blood knot is essentially two clinch knots tied back-to-back. The two strands of material are crossed, each tag end is wrapped several times around the standing portion of the other strand, and then the ends are tucked back through the opening formed by the original crossing of the strands and trapped by the wraps drawn down tightly. The knot sounds more complicated than it is.

Like the clinch knot, the strength of the blood knot is influenced by the number of turns involved. I like to use five-turn blood knots for the tippet and for the last couple of strands in the taper section of the leader (more information on that later in the chapter). Four- and three-turn knots seem enough for the butt section of the leader. In mono of large diameter, the five-turn knots are hard to draw up neatly and tightly, and the leader isn't likely to break there anyway, so the maximum knot strength isn't really needed.

The blood knot and both of the clinch knots draw up more smoothly and are more reliable if you moisten the strands with saliva before tying them. A little extra saliva on the knot as it is being drawn tight helps to prevent scorching of the material, which might weaken the knot. I have also developed the habit of capturing the free ends of the blood knot in my teeth while drawing up the knot. Otherwise the strands may pull out unless you leave so much excess that you're really wasting material.

- *Advantages:* The blood knot is a strong connection that maintains a straight-line relationship between two pieces of monofilament, and it doesn't waste much mono. It can be tied with two relatively short strands of material and can be clipped close without weakening. Very importantly, the waste material left after completing the knot stands out at right angles to the knot itself. So a long strand of intentionally left "waste" can be used as a "dropper" for fishing an extra fly or for attaching split shot, which can then be removed without disturbing the fly.

• *Disadvantage:* The only real drawback of the blood knot is that it is reliable only when used to join strands of similar diameter. If the strands are more than 0.003 inch different in diameter, the knot tends to slip. The only way of overcoming this limitation—I forgot this too the night I lost that big bass—is to double the small strand and then tie the knot as usual. If the doubled small strand nearly matches the diameter of the large strand, the knot will be reliable.

Surgeon's Knot

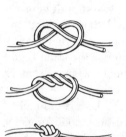

Figure 5–5
The surgeon's knot

This one I'll never forget again. It is a simple overhand knot, tied through the same loop twice (see Figure 5–5). For even greater strength, the material can be passed through the loop three times, creating the "triple" surgeon's knot.

• *Advantages:* The surgeon's knot is simple to tie—most anglers find it simpler than the blood knot. A strong and compact knot, it can be used to join sections of material that are widely different in diameter. The surgeon's knot is essential for making the short, rapidly tapering leaders used with sinking fly lines.
• *Disadvantages:* The knot has only a few, but sometimes important, shortcomings. Because the strands must be oriented in opposite directions, and because one must be passed entirely through the loop, at least that one must be fairly long and unattached to anything else. For example, the surgeon's knot does not lend itself to attaching backing to fly line, because either the entire fly line or the backing and reel would have to be passed through the loop. I also find that the surgeon's knot wastes more material than the blood knot. Finally, since the waste does not stand out at right angles to the knot, trimming it close is a little difficult, and it does not lend itself to use for droppers. Still, the usefulness of the surgeon's knot makes it more and more popular. I find myself using it often, now that I've learned the hard way how to tie it.

Tube Knot

Known also as the "nail knot" and, in a more elaborate version, as the "needle knot," this is the basic knot for attaching the leader to the fly line, and it can also be used for attaching backing. I'm recommending the tube version because I think it's the easiest to tie.

Refer to Figure 5–6. The end of the fly line is oriented in one direction, the leader butt end in the other, and the tube between them. The leader butt is wrapped around the fly line, the tube, and itself at least five times. The end is then passed through the tube and back out the opening formed by the first of the wraps. The tube is withdrawn, and

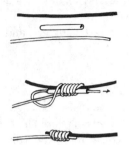

Figure 5–6
The tube knot

the coiled wraps are held together while the two ends of the monofilament are gradually pulled tight. As the coils tighten up, greater pressure can be exerted on them to keep them in alignment. A little saliva helps them draw up smoothly and tightly.

If it sounds like you need four hands to tie the tube knot, that's not far from the truth, at least on your first few attempts. But it becomes easier as you practice. And if a couple of the wraps overlap each other as you pull them tight, it really won't much affect the security of the knot.

Many anglers like to coat their tube knots with a heavy waterproof glue, such as Pliobond, after tying. This not only adds to the security of the knot, but also helps to streamline it so that it will slip through the guides of the rod easily. Several coats are usually required to create the streamlined effect.

If you don't have a tube handy for the knot, you can use the little plastic tube on which cotton swabs are attached. Just clip off the cotton ends, leaving a tube of the desired length. Any tube you use should be smooth, so the monofilament slides through it easily and so it can be withdrawn without disturbing the knot. Also, the smaller the tube to begin with, the less the knot has to be drawn down after the tube is pulled out.

Some anglers don't like the slight offset between line and leader that the tube knot involves. I don't think it makes any difference, but if you care about such things you can use the needle knot version. To do so, insert a needle big enough to make a hole through which your leader butt can go into the end of the fly line, and then out the side of the line an inch or so back from the very end. (Heating the needle slightly makes it slide through easier, but don't overdo it.) Then slide the leader butt through the end of the line before tying the tube knot as described. You now have a connection in which the leader butt comes directly out of the fly line.

The tube knot is complicated enough that you don't want to be tying them all the time. Many anglers simply tie a permanent, short section of heavy monofilament to their line with a tube knot, and then tie the butt section of their leader to that with a blood knot. Or you can place one loop in the end of the leader butt and another in the end of the permanent mono section attached to the fly line. Then loop the two together, and you need no knots to change leaders. Whatever system you favor, choose one that allows you to change leaders on the stream without fuss. The tube knot is one to tie at home, under comfortable circumstances, rather than on the stream. And if you opt for one of the alternate systems described, one tube knot may suffice for the life of the fly line.

I have tried to keep this list of knots to the absolute minimum, and I'm certain that experienced anglers would say that I've left out some important ones. But these are the essential ones for the beginner, and, since I've burdened you with so few, I'm going to badger you once more: Learn these knots and practice them until you are totally familiar with them. You'll need to make an investment in time and money to get started in fly fishing, and you don't want to lose your first good fish to a faulty knot. Remember, reliable knots are tied by relaxed anglers, and relaxation comes with practice and confidence.

Leaders

I had an object lesson in the importance of leaders about six years ago, when my friend Ralph Schmidt called one day. Now lots of people have twinkles in their eyes. But Ralph has one in his voice, too, especially when he's talking about fly fishing, and even more so when he's setting me up for a fall. "I know where there's a big fish," he said. He paused here to whet my appetite. "I'd tell you except you wouldn't land him and then you'd only be disappointed . . ." Needless to say, I rose like a hungry brook trout, "Tell you what, Ralph. Spare me your concern for my mental health, and just tell me where the fish is." Of course, Ralph allowed me to weasel the fish's location out of him, as he had planned to do all along, and a couple of hours later I was on the small Pennsylvania stream that Ralph and I often fish together.

Sure enough, the trout was just where Ralph had said it would be. And I could see why he was so confident I couldn't land it. The fish's feeding location was just under one of the trailing roots of an old tree that had been blown over by a summer storm. It was obvious that once hooked, it would immediately head for the snag. Suddenly the picture was clear: Ralph had hooked this fish and lost it, and he wanted me to have the same humiliating experience. Nevertheless, I couldn't resist. The fish was a beautiful brown trout, about seventeen inches, and I rigged up with fumbling fingers, tying my favorite all-purpose dry fly, size 16, to a 4X tippet.

The first cast fell true, and the fly drifted down just to the left of the root under which the fish lay. The flutter of fins betrayed the fish's interest, but it made no move toward the fly. A couple of casts made it clear that this fish wasn't going to be moved by a 4X tippet.

My doubts growing, I added a strand of 5X, reknotted the fly, and pitched a cast upstream again. This time the fish came out from under the snag and studied the fly for several feet before rejecting it with a scornful shrug. That was on the first cast. No succeeding cast could elicit any additional interest.

The die was cast. I retrieved line, clipped off the fly, and added a length of 6X tippet, reducing my margin to a pound-and-a-half of strain. Sure enough, on the first cast with that 6X tippet, the trout rose and took the fly as if it had been feeding on Hare's Ear dries all day.

I set the hook, and the trout, as I knew it would, ran under the snarled roots of the old tree, stretching my leader over one of the roots in the process. I knew that I couldn't pull the fish out of there; my tackle was too frail for that. So I decided to see if I could fool the fish into thinking there was no connection between us. Maybe then it would swim out of its own accord and we could do battle on more equal terms.

So I gave slack and laid the rod down on the bank, lit my pipe and waited. Ten minutes later I was beginning to wonder if this strategy would work. After twenty minutes my pipe was cold, my temper was warm, and the fish was still holding carefully in the roots of the tree, my leader still stretched precariously behind it and over a twisted root.

I tried tightening up on the trout again, applying moderate, worrying pressure. I strummed the line, hoping that the irritating vibrations would anger the trout into swimming out into open water. I even tossed small pebbles into the snag, but the only result was to urge the trout deeper into the morass of roots.

Finally, I knew I had two choices. I could sit there, attached to this fish all day and then break off in the evening so I could take my rod home. Or I could break off now and fish for the rest of the afternoon. I chose the latter, and when I did, then and only then did the fish come out of the snag, parading past with my fly still in its jaw. I sensed that I could detect a smile very much like Ralph Schmidt's on its face.

You won't fly fish for long before discovering that your leader has a profound effect on how many fish you can interest, how many you hook, and how many you land. In fact, under many circumstances, the leader is more important to success than the fly.

The leader, you will recall, has two purposes: attachment and detachment. It attaches the fly to the fly line, while at the same time detaching it from the line with a length of clear monofilament. To accomplish these two purposes, the leader must be tapered from a large portion which is attached to the line to a small tippet to which the fly is tied.

Tapered Leaders

Tapered leaders are available either in the *single-strand type*, which is chemically tapered, or the *knotted type*, in which several sections of nylon are knotted together to form the tapered leader. Both are available commercially, although the knotless types are easier to find outside of specialty fly shops, and the knotted leader can be home-made. Each type has its advantages, but most anglers tie at least some of their own leaders, although they may use the knotless type on occasion as well.

I have suggested that you get started in fly fishing with the store-bought chemically tapered leaders. Eventually, if you stay interested in fly fishing, you may want to begin making your own leaders. Doing so has a number of advantages:

- *Cost:* You can tie leaders at home for much less than you pay for them in the store. A leader-tying kit, which costs about as much as ten or twelve commercial leaders, will tie about two or three times that many with you supplying the labor.
- *Versatility:* Your own leaders can be made to fit your particular casting style and the special conditions you face on the water that you fish. The extremes of leader length and taper, such as the three-foot tapered leader you might need to fish with a deep sinking line or the sixteen-footer you might want for late summer dry fly fishing, are either unavailable or hard to find commercially. If you want them, you have to make them yourself.
- *Variety:* With home-tied leaders you can afford to carry a wide selection of lengths and tapers, wider than you could justify if you were paying a dollar or more for each of them.
- *Practice:* If you tie your own leaders, you get a lot of relaxed practice with the blood knot, and probably with the surgeon's knot too. With practice will come speed, confidence, and skill in tying these knots.

Leader Formulas

For a tapered leader to perform well, it must be designed so the flow of power from the cast is transmitted from the line into the leader and carried throughout the leader's length in a smooth progression. That power must finally turn the fly over and set it down on target. A poorly designed leader, or one not suited for the fly being cast, will collapse in a pile on the surface.

Generally speaking, a competent fly caster can turn over any leader in which each strand, from butt to tippet, is shorter than the preceding one. A good leader design, however, is one in which the taper steps down in increments of about 0.002, and in which the proportions of the leader correspond to the 60–20–20 formula. This is a leader with:

- 60-percent butt (several long strands of relatively stiff nylon)
- 20-percent taper (a few short strands of rapidly decreasing diameter), and
- 20-percent tippet (a single long strand of soft, flexible nylon, to which the fly is attached).

Table 5–1 is reproduced from the leader formulas supplied by one of the major tackle companies with its leader tying kit. If you check these formulas with your calculator, you'll see that they generally follow the 60–20–20 design. I've used these formulas for years (with an occasional slight modification), and I'm sure they will suit your needs, too.

Many anglers find that they need slightly different performance from that of the standard formulas. Three ways to experiment with these leader formulas involve modifications of the butt, taper, and tippet.

Table 5–1   Leader Formulas

Specifications: 7½' Tapered Trout Leaders

0X	1X	2X	3X	4X
24" – .019"	24" – .019"	24" – .019"	24" – .019"	24" – .019"
16" – .017"	16" – .017"	16" – .017"	16" – .017"	16" – .017"
14" – .015"	14" – .015"	14" – .015"	14" – .015"	14" – .015"
9" – .013"	9" – .013"	9" – .013"	6" – .013"	6" – .013"
9" – .012"	9" – .011"	9" – .011"	6" – .011"	6" – .011"
18" – .011"	18" – .010"	18" – .009"	6" – .009"	6" – .009"
			18" – .008"	18" – .007"

Specifications: 9' Tapered Trout Leaders

0X	1X	2X	3X	4X	5X
36" – .021"	36" – .021"	36" – .021"	36" – .021"	36" – .021"	28" – .021
16" – .019"	16" – .019"	16" – .019"	16" – .019"	16" – .019"	14" – .019
12" – .017"	12" – .017"	12" – .017"	12" – .017"	12" – .017"	12" – .017
8" – .015"	8" – .015"	8" – .015	6" – .015"	6" – .015"	10" – .015
8" – .013"	8" – .013"	8" – .013"	6" – .013"	6" – .013"	6" – .013
8" – .012"	8" – .012"	8" – .011"	6" – .011"	6" – .011"	6" – .011
20" – .011"	20" – .010"	20" – .009"	6" – .009"	6" – .009"	6" – .009
			20" – .008"	20" – .007"	6" – .007
					20" – .006

Specifications: 12' Tapered Trout Leaders

4X	5X	6X	7X
36" – .021"	36" – .021"	36" – .021"	28" – .021
24" – .019"	24" – .019"	24" – .019"	18" – .019
16" – .017"	16" – .017"	16" – .017"	16" – .017
12" – .015"	12" – .015"	12" – .015"	14" – .015
7" – .013"	7" – .013"	7" – .013"	12" – .013
7" – .011"	7" – .011"	7" – .011"	7" – .011
7" – .009"	7" – .009"	7" – .009"	7" – .009
7" – .008"	7" – .008"	7" – .007"	7" – .007
28" – .007"	28" – .006"	28" – .005"	7" – .005
			28" – .004

Specifications: 7½' Saltwater, Salmon, Steelhead, Bass Bug Leaders

Extra Light	Light	Medium	Heavy	Extra Heavy
.021 – .011	.021 – .013	.021 – .015	.021 – .017	.023 – .019
18" – .021	26" – .021	26" – .021	36" – .021	36" – .023
16" – .019	22" – .019	23" – .019	34" – .019	34" – .021
14" – .017	12" – .017	21" – .017	20" – .017	20" – .019
12" – .015	10" – .015	20" – .015		
10" – .013	20" – .013			
20" – .011				

Specifications: 9' Saltwater, Salmon, Steelhead, Bass Bug Leaders

Extra Light	Light	Medium	Heavy	Extra Heavy
.021 – .011	.021 – .013	.021 – .015	.021 – .017	.023 – .019
22" – .021	32" – .021	40" – .021	46" – .021	46" – .023
20" – .019	28" – .019	26" – .019	42" – .019	42" – .021
18" – .017	16" – .017	22" – .017	20" – .017	20" – .019
16" – .015	12" – .015	20" – .015		
12" – .013	20" – .013			
20" – .011				

Courtesy The Orvis Company

BUTT. The diameter of the butt section should be determined ultimately by the diameter and stiffness of the fly line. Ordinarily, leaders with butts about two-thirds the diameter of the fly line work well. Yet since fly lines differ in diameter and leader materials differ in stiffness, you may have to experiment to find the ideal butt diameter for a particular line.

One way to assess the relative stiffness of the two materials is to grasp the fly line in one hand and the leader butt in the other, with the knot joining them equidistant between your hands. Now push the two sections together slightly and observe the curve that they form. If the curve is even and smooth, with the knot in the center, then the stiffness of the two materials is about the same. You may assume that butt diameter will work well with that line. If the curve is more pronounced on the line side of the connection, the butt material is too stiff and a smaller diameter will work better. If the curve is more pronounced on the leader side of the knot, the butt is too limp and a larger diameter will give better performance.

I have found that most of my lines of 4- and 5-weight cast well with leaders with butt sections of 0.019, and my lines of 7-weight and heavier almost all work best with leaders butted with 0.021 or 0.023. Six-weight lines work with either 0.019 or 0.021. Still, there are exceptions. I own a tapered 6-weight line of British manufacture that works best with a leader butt of only 0.015!

TAPER. The rapidly graduated section of the leader is where the taper speeds up at the same time that the strands of material are getting shorter. The performance of a leader can be altered significantly by small changes in the lengths of these strands. So shortening the strands in this section speeds up the flow of power through the leader, transmitting the power of the cast more smartly into the tippet section. Lengthening these strands slows down the power transmission. If you have trouble turning over and straightening your leader, try shortening these sections an inch at a time until the problem is solved. If your leader is turning over too hard, lengthening these strands will probably correct it.

TIPPET. You might wish to lengthen your tippet—or shorten it under certain conditions—beyond the dimension offered in the standard formulas for a number of reasons. A long tippet allows a more natural drift of the fly because it is more supple and also because it tends to pile up slightly on the cast, landing in a series of little curves that give the fly the freedom to drift naturally. Also, a longer tippet is more elastic than a short one, so lengthening a very light tippet helps to keep you from breaking off fish. On the other hand, a long tippet is hard to handle in the wind, and it is difficult to manage when fishing large, air-resistant flies. Under those conditions, you'll find a shorter tippet more desirable.

Knotless Leaders

Finally, although we've talked about most hand-tied leaders, don't overlook the virtues of the knotless type. Sometimes the single-strand leader is better. One particular instance is when fishing weedy waters where vegetation tends to pile up on the leader knots of a tied leader. Also, many anglers are now adopting a compromise between the hand-tied and the chemically tapered leader. They buy the knotless type, then add a heavier butt section and a lighter tippet. This combination provides many of the advantages of both types, with only two knots to tie.

Leader Length and Tippet Size

Deciding what leader to use before actually assessing a fishing situation can be difficult, but you can follow some general guidelines. Small stream fishing usually involves short casts and relatively slow line speed, so turning over a really long leader is hard under these conditions. A seven- or eight-foot leader is good here. When fishing under extremely difficult conditions, over spooky fish, you might want to go to nine or ten feet, but you could add a long tippet to your eight-foot leader and still be in good shape. I've rarely found it necessary to fish a leader longer than twelve feet.

At the other extreme, you need a shorter leader for sinking lines because the leader tends to be buoyed up by the water, defeating the purpose of the line. Five-foot leaders are about right with most sink-tip lines, and I go as short as three feet with extra-fast sinkers. Recent experiments indicate that sinking line leaders can be as short as a few inches without spooking fish.

Selecting tippet size can be critical. Many anglers rely on the rule of four: The fly size should be four times the size of the tippet. Thus a #12 fly would call for a 3X tippet. Like most such formulas, however, this one is often inadequate, especially in fishing the dry fly. Experiments at Penn State by George Harvey and Joe Humphreys have shown that the ideal dry fly tippet is one that falls on the surface in a series of smooth curves. Such a tippet allows the fly to drift without deviating from the speed and direction of other material floating in the same current. This deviation, called *drag*, is death to angling success with sophisticated fish.

Since each fly has a different density and air resistance, each requires a different length and diameter of tippet to perform properly.

Experimentation is the only way to achieve the perfect tippet with a given dry fly. Remember, however, that length is often more critical in a tippet than diameter. Contrary to what many people believe, small diameter tippets are not invisible. You can demonstrate this to yourself in a swimming pool or even with a glass of water. Even 8X material, a tiny .003-inch in diameter, is plainly visible in clear water. What matters in a tippet is suppleness, and if you construct it properly you can create a drag-free tippet without going to ridiculously small monofilament. By using sensibly sized tippets you can land more fish and avoid harming them by playing them for excessive periods. Had I known this a few years ago, I might have lengthened my 5X tippet and held that trout out of the snag.

Incidentally, you might be interested in another "magic number" for simplifying the relationship between the X designation and diameter. The formula is based on the number eleven: Subtract the X designation from eleven, and you have the diameter that X is supposed to be. Thus 3X is 0.008. If you keep these two numbers in mind—four for matching fly to tippet and eleven for relating X to diameter—much of the apparent complexity of leader decisions can be minimized.

Table 5–2 shows the approximate breaking strength in pounds for the various sizes of leader material. The actual breaking strength varies somewhat according to the manufacturer, the knots employed, and other factors, so these figures are only rough guidelines.

If this chapter has seemed complicated to you, don't be intimidated. Remember that you're going to start with two knotless tapered leaders, and you'll do fine with them. As you become expert enough to discover their limitations, the information in this chapter may help you to go beyond those limitations. Above all, practice those knots!

Table 5–2   Approximate Breaking Strength of Monofilament

X Designation	Diameter	Approved Pounds Test
8X	0.003	0.75
7X	0.004	1
6X	0.005	1.5
5X	0.006	2.5
4X	0.007	3
3X	0.008	3.8
2X	0.009	4.5
1X	0.010	5.5
0X	0.011	6.5
	0.012	7.5
	0.013	8.5
	0.014	10
	0.015	11.5
	0.016	13.5
	0.017	15
	0.019	20
	0.021	24

Recommended Books

Fishing Knots by Lefty Kreh and Mark Sosin (Crown Publishers, Inc., 1972). This is the bible of the knot crowd, and deservedly so. It contains complete directions for tying all the necessary fishing knots for fly fishing and other fishing methods. Particularly good is the section on knots for saltwater fly fishing. Don't head for salt water with your fly rod without checking them out.

6
THE AQUATIC ENVIRONMENT

The big day has finally arrived. You've bought a balanced fly casting outfit and practiced in your yard until you can hit your hat at thirty feet. You have a few flies, which have been recommended by local anglers, and your vest contains the first installment of what will become a trove of gadgets and paraphernalia. You walk clumsily in your new boots, and your feet are beginning to perspire already. You've been thinking about this venture for weeks, and now you're at the water.

What do you do now.

The answers to that question (there is no single answer) depend on two things: your understanding of the water that you are going to fish and the fish that you expect to find there. This understanding does not have to be deep or complex, and it will never be complete. But to get off to a good start, you need to know something not only about fish, but also about the aquatic environment that they inhabit and share with other creatures.

The Fish

A fish is a highly specialized animal, designed by evolution to fit the special demands of a water environment. Although it seems too obvious to mention, a liquid environment is far different from the gas environment that you and I occupy, and those differences are reflected in every aspect of the fish's anatomy and behavior. To become an effective fly fisherman you should know a few general principles about fish and their functioning.

Perception

Perception (defined by most psychologists as sensation plus interpretation) takes place under water as well as in the air. Fish are able to perceive their world acutely, as fishermen who have had their carefully-tied flies rejected can tell you. The water environment, however, has some special characteristics that influence perception.

VISION. Even the clearest water is far more turbid than air, so the eye of the fish does not have to discern detail at great distances. In our terms, fish are nearsighted, but within their visual range they can make precise observations. Many studies show that gamefish can discriminate colors and sizes with a high degree of accuracy. Each of these attributes is of great importance to the fly fisherman.

Due to the location of their eyes, most freshwater fish can see much of what is behind them as well as what is in front. Due to the angle at which the light bends when entering water, a fish can see everything above the surface, but all this visual stimulation is compressed into a small area called the *window*, a cone-shaped opening to the above-water world that the fish carries about with it. We'll have more to say about the window in our discussion of dry fly fishing, but for now remember that the size of the window changes with the fish's depth under the surface. Except for the small portion that is in the window, the surface is a mirror to the fish, reflecting the bottom and its features.

HEARING. Although gamefish have ears, most of the fish's "hearing" is done by the *lateral line*, a nerve system along both sides of the fish, at the midline. The lateral line is sensitive to vibrations in the water. Contrary to what many anglers believe, sounds carry well under water, especially low-frequency sounds. So careless wading or other subsurface disturbances can alarm fish at a considerable distance. Noises made above the surface, such as conversation, will not be heard by the fish unless some vehicle, such as the bottom of a boat, conducts the vibrations into the water.

SMELL. Although fly fishermen have not figured out how to make use of this fact, many species of gamefish are quite sensitive to odors. Anadromous fishes, which return to fresh water to spawn, find their way back to their native streams by smell. Unlike humans, who must sniff vigorously to smell faint odors, fish constantly have a supply of water flowing past their olfactory nerve endings, and so they are sampling the odors of their environment continuously.

TASTE. Fish are sensitive to taste, although the fly angler must concede an advantage to the live bait fisherman in this department. We can, however, avoid presenting the fish with taste sensations known to be offensive to them, such as petroleum-based products. One reason for using aerosol insect repellents is that they can be applied without getting the product on your hands. Many anglers believe that a thorough handwashing before handling flies is a good idea.

Motivation

Any fish in any water is governed by a single overriding instinct: survival. This global instinct is manifested through three motives that govern most of the day-to-day behavior of the fish: protection, hunger, and comfort. The drive to reproduce is stronger than any of these at times, but since it has only a seasonal impact we will disregard it here.

PROTECTION. Protection is the highest priority of the fish, and it will sacrifice both comfort and feeding opportunities, at least for a time, to be safe. Fish spend their lives trying to escape predators, and the majority fail. When they are still only eggs, they may be eaten by mature fish, and they may be subject to cannibalism by larger members of their own species when they are fry. Many fry and even mature fish are also lost to herons, ospreys, kingfishers and fish-eating ducks. Even after reaching maturity, fish are still subject to predation by many animals, including man. So fish learn to be alert to danger from the world above the water. Little wonder that protection is the first concern of a fish.

To a fish, protection means cover. Fish will remain close to a safe area where they can flee at the first sign of danger. In a trout stream a safe place means stream bed rocks or undercut banks that provide shelter. In a bass river, a downed tree or a nearby weed bed into which a fish can race if predators threaten may provide underwater protection. Finally, cover may be a deep water area; a mature fish is safe in the depths from most predators. Whatever the source of cover, a fish that has survived to maturity will never be far from it.

HUNGER. Next to protection, feeding opportunities are paramount. A stream fish seeks a location in or near a current that carries food morsels past it on a regular basis. A river fish forages, seeking a meal of smaller fish. A lake fish follows schools of baitfish as they move about or searches for crayfish in the rocky shallows.

A feeding fish usually has to sacrifice some measure of protection to feed, and the extent of the sacrifice varies with the richness of the environment. A brook trout in a relatively barren mountain stream may have to accept large risks to feed, while a brown trout in a rich limestone creek may be able to feed in weed beds so thick and full of forage that it is nearly as well protected as when seeking shelter alone. Under most circumstances, however, a feeding fish is more vulnerable to predation than a fish that is not feeding. Feeding fish, therefore, are cautious fish.

COMFORT. Comfort has several meanings in the fish's world. Often comfort means current relief, a respite from the incessant flow of the stream. Like protection and feeding opportunities, current relief is a matter of degree. It is not usually possible for a stream fish to achieve total current relief without giving up most feeding opportunities or accepting exposure to danger. The need for current relief varies with the species. A streamlined trout can hold easily in a current that would soon exhaust a chunky bluegill. Generally, then, an active stream fish seeks a measure of current relief consistent with its other motives rather than an absolute elimination of the flow's pressure.

Many stream locations and features provide current relief. Rocks provide sheltering areas both downstream and upstream of their location. Water is less swift at the bottom of the stream than at the surface because the friction of water moving over it slows the flow as compared with the top. Also, various areas of the stream may offer diminished current speed when compared with the main flow. Areas where the gradient—the slope—of the streambed is temporarily moderated become pools, offering far less current stress than the riffles in between. The favorite areas of feeding fish are protected locations just out of the main current flow, where the fish can hold close enough to move into the current to intercept a passing food item. Even actively feeding fish will do so in the most comfortable area possible.

Experienced anglers become adept at "reading the water." This is the skill of detecting those locations where fish are or should be found. By now you should be alert to a number of stream features that may provide cover or a comfortable feeding lie for a fish, and you should look for such places when you are astream. Another source of potential information about fish lies is the surface of the water. If you watch small bits of floating material, leaf matter, foam, and such, you will soon see the areas where relatively quiet water borders on food-carrying currents. Finally, in your fishing of a stream, you will catch some fish, spook others, and spot still more that you do not disturb. Note these locations carefully (carrying a small notebook can be a help), because unless the stream changes drastically these same locations will continue to harbor fish in the future.

Temperature comfort is another motive of fish that has major implications. Fish are cold-blooded animals; their body temperature and rate of metabolism fluctuate with the temperature of the water they live in. When the water becomes cold, all their body processes slow down drastically. At the other extreme, when the water becomes too warm, the metabolism of the fish accelerates rapidly, sometimes to a fatal level.

Temperature is also important because warm water has less dissolved oxygen than cool water. High water temperatures, then, deal fish a double blow: While the heat speeds up their body processes, the lowered oxygen content deprives them of sufficient respiratory capacity to support their increased metabolism.

Table 6–1 shows the maximum tolerable temperatures and the preferred temperature ranges for a number of gamefish that interest fly anglers. Generally speaking, feeding is most intense during periods when water temperature is at the cooler end of the preferred range. Remember, too, that water temperature not only affects fish, but it also controls the behavior of the other aquatic organisms that make up their diet. No wonder that aquatic biologists agree that water temperature is the single most important variable in predicting the behavior of fish.

Table 6–1 Water Temperature and Gamefish Activity

Species	Upper Limit of Toleration	Preferred Range (Fahrenheit)
Rainbow Trout	80°	55–65°
Brown Trout	84°	55–62°
Brook Trout	77°	55–63°
Largemouth Bass	High 90s	60–80°
Smallmouth Bass	High 90s	60–75°

Now you know why that stream thermometer recommended in Chapter 4 is so important. By taking the water temperature you can make predictions about where fish should be and what sort of behavior to expect from them. If you are seeking, say, rainbow trout but find the temperature higher than they prefer, then look for them in the riffle areas where water turbulence aerates the flow and adds additional dissolved oxygen. Better yet, use your thermometer to locate spring holes where the temperature is substantially cooler than the rest of the stream. The fish will be there.

Remember, then, that fish are governed by the survival instinct, which means protection, food, and comfort. If some location in the fish's environment provides all three of these elements, the fish will be found in this *prime lie*. If not, the fish will choose a location that offers protection and feeding opportunities at reduced comfort if it is hungry or a location that offers protection and comfort with fewer feeding opportunities if it is not.

You have probably heard it said that particularly successful anglers catch a lot of fish because they have learned to "think like a trout" or to "think like a bass." This is nonsense. An angler who thought like a fish could not even find the water, much less fish it successfully.

Fish *do not think*, at least not in the sense that we use the word. Their brains are not designed for analysis or decision making. Fish are successful organisms because they respond to the demands of their environment *without thinking*. Those that cannot do so successfully die, while those who succeed pass their adaptable characteristics along to subsequent generations.

This is not to say that fish cannot learn. Indeed they can, and gamefish in particular show rapid learning, especially of avoidance responses in the face of fishing pressure. But the learning of fish is mechanical; their responses can be conditioned, but they have little capacity to store information or to generalize from previous learning in new situations. They can learn, but they cannot *know*.

Successful fly fishermen study the fish's environment because that environment *controls* the fish's behavior. If you can begin to understand what controls the behavior of the fish, then you are in a position to *predict* that behavior. Considered in this light, each cast an angler makes is a prediction that is either confirmed or rejected by the response of the fish.

We will never develop a fool-proof fishing system (thank goodness) because the environment is too complex and too rapidly changing. Still, when fly fishermen are successful, they are because they have presented the fish with an artificial morsel under conditions that the fish perceives to be natural and nonthreatening. The fact that we often accomplish this by accident as well as by design does not diminish the accuracy of the analysis.

Our natural tendency is to conclude that fish are "smart" when we can't catch them. The truth, however, is just the opposite. When we can't catch them, it's because they are *not smart*. The fish are, without thinking, instinctively rejecting our inferior imitation of an environmental stimulus. If it were really a battle of wits between man and fish, all the fish would have been caught long ago.

The Water

How the fish meets its needs and how the angler locates the quarry both depend on the type of water the fish occupies. In lakes, fish seek a depth that meets the need for comfortable temperature while offering feeding opportunities, or they hold at a comfortable depth during the bright hours and move to shallower waters in the evening to feed. In rivers that are subject to temperature elevation during the hot months, this same phenomenon may be observed. Remember, too, that depth is protection to a fish. So when the sun is high and the shadows short, the fish's need for protection is particularly acute.

Another important factor is the acidity or alkalinity of the water. Trout streams and bass rivers, as well as lakes and impoundments, provide environments of varying quality depending on the chemical characteristics of the water.

Freestone Streams

Most mountain trout streams and many bass rivers fall into the class called "freestone streams" by fly anglers. These streams, fed primarily by surface runoff, are subject to flooding and drought. In the upper elevations they have a considerable gradient and typically show the riffle-pool sequence that the trout fisherman knows so well. Freestone streams are acid, sometimes decidedly so, and for this reason they are not very fertile in producing the aquatic life that fish can use for food. And since runoff water provides most of the flow in a freestone stream, the water temperatures fluctuate widely and may be ideal for fish only during certain periods of the year.

Figure 6–1 The author fishes a typical freestone stream in the low-water period of early fall (Photo by Katherine G. Lee)

Although freestone streams are beautiful and favored by many fly anglers, they can be tough environments for fish. Because of temperature variations and marginal forage, growth may be slow and restricted to a few months of the year. The steep gradients of many freestone streams require fish to fight the current to feed. The fish must devote much of the energy gained from food intake to just hold the feeding position. A fish in such circumstances must feed more often and for longer periods, and so it is subject to predation more regularly.

Many freestone streams, which are already marginal environments, are being further degraded by man. Timbering in the watershed raises water temperature, increases flooding and siltation, and reduces the capacity of the aquifer to hold moisture against drought periods. Acid seepage from strip mines or deep mines introduces additional, often fatal, acid loads into the stream. And these degrading influences not only penalize fish already in the stream, but also interfere with reproduction and diminish other aquatic life.

Limestone Streams

These streams get their name because they are found in parts of the country with extensive limestone deposits. Limestone streams have their origins in underground rivers rather than in runoff. They usually

Figure 6–2 A classic limestone stream—the Letort. The angler is Pennsylvania's Ed Shenk. (Photo by the the author)

begin where an underground stream comes to the surface, and sometimes they disappear in the same way. Limestone streams are alkaline, and they carry a high load of minerals and nutrients from their underground passage through limestone rock.

These streams offer a much richer environment than do freestone streams. Much of the history and traditions of fly fishing was played out on English "chalk" streams, limestoners by another name. The high nutrient content of these waters promotes weed growth, which in turn provides cover for fish and for many types of aquatic insects and crustaceans on which fish feed. Because they usually have only one major source, limestone streams are generally more stable than freestone. In most of these streams flooding is rare, and the temperature is consistent the whole year. In many limestone creeks the food supply is so abundant that fish have the luxury either of feeding at leisurely intervals or of eating a continuous but slow banquet under nearly impenetrable weed cover. And since most limestone streams are valley streams, their modest gradient eliminates the need for fish to expend energy fighting heavy currents. All these advantages, plus year-round growth, explains why so many trophy fish come out of limestone streams.

Limestone streams are not free of problems, however, and again the culprit is man. Limestone country is fertile country, and many of these creeks flow through agricultural land. They are thus subject to taint by insecticides, herbicides, and fertilizers. Some of the most famous of these streams are in areas now undergoing heavy development, with road building, housing projects, and sewer lines along their banks.

Excessive weed growth is often a problem too. Encouraged by leaching fertilizers, rampant weed growth displaces the water and spreads it outward, turning firm banks into marshy bogs and rotting the roots of trees that shield the stream from sunlight. The dead trees fall into the stream, displacing still more water and admitting still more sunlight, which in turn promotes more weed growth and continues to raise the water temperature. Although limestone creeks are the richest environment for fish, they are also among the most delicate.

Due to the important differences between freestone and limestone streams, they require slightly different fishing approaches. That's a topic we'll return to when we consider the fishing techniques with various types of flies.

Fish Food

Many aquatic organisms share the water with the fish, and most of them are fish food at one stage of development or another. We'll look at several types.

Aquatic insects are the backbone of fly fishing. The beginning fly fisher should know something about three major groups of insects: the mayflies, the caddisflies, and the stoneflies. Although these insects share some similar features, their differences are most critical from the standpoint of the angler.

MAYFLIES. Probably a mayfly was the first fly that an angler tried to represent. Even today a majority of fly patterns are attempts to imitate mayflies in various stages of development.

The mayflies (there are about 500 species in North America) belong to the order *Ephemeroptera*, which means "living but a day." Actually, a mayfly's life is longer than a day, but most species live as winged creatures for only a day or so. Mayflies begin life as eggs laid at the surface of the water, which then drop to the bottom and stick to stones and to other material on the streambed.

The eggs develop into nymphs. Although there is considerable variation in color and size among the various species, there are four broad types of mayfly nymphs:

Figure 6–3
A mayfly dun

1. *The clingers* have a pronounced flat shape. They live in fast, well aerated water where they cling to the bottoms of stones.
2. *The burrowers* spend most of their nymphal stage in silt or fine gravel on the stream bottom. They are more often found in quiet water and are common in lakes and slow, meandering streams. They are recognized by prominent tusks on their heads.
3. *The crawlers* are oval in cross-section and spend their lives as nymphs clambering around the stream bottom.
4. *The swimmers* are streamlined. They swim freely about gathering food.

Most mayfly nymphs have three tails (the clinger group has many exceptions), gills along their abdomens, and a prominent bulge in the thorax area (the part to which the legs are attached). This bulge is the wing pads, and they darken as the insects prepare to emerge. During the year or so that most species remain in the nymphal stage they go through several molts or *instars*, during which they shed their skeletons as they grow larger. (Insects have their skeletons on the outside, remember.)

Finally, at the time of emergence the nymphs migrate to the surface, their skeletons split open at the thorax, and a winged insect crawls out. This creature is called a *subimago* by entomologists, a *dun* by fly fishermen. The duns usually ride the surface for a time until their wings are dry enough for flight, and during this time they are very vulnerable to fish. The emergence process is called a *hatch* by fly anglers

95

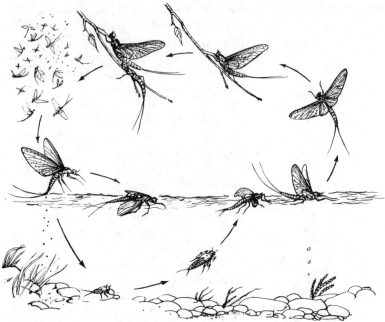

Figure 6–4 The mayfly life cycle: From the lower left, the nymph rises from the bottom. The dun (subimago) emerges, flies to a nearby tree, and molts into the spinner (imago). It then joins the mating swarm, after which the fertilized females lay eggs in the stream (ovipositing). Finally, both sexes die.

everywhere. Duns can be identified by the fact that they have opaque wings. A few species have splotches of dark coloration on the wings. The wings of mayflies are easy to observe because they are carried upright over the body when the insect is at rest. Mayflies are the only insects that carry their wings in this sail-like posture, so they are easy to differentiate from other insects.

Those duns that escape the fish fly off the surface, clumsily at first. And, if they are not eaten by birds (who can get as excited by a hatch as the fish), they fly to a streamside tree or bush. There they alight, usually on the underside of a leaf. Within a few hours they shed their dun skins and become sexually mature adults called *imagoes*.

The imago, called a *spinner* by fly anglers, is recognized readily by its translucent wing. Imagoes also usually have larger eyes than duns, as well as longer tails and front legs; the females often show egg sacs at the rear of their abdomens. Some hours after the original hatch (around a day in most species), the spinners of both sexes return to the stream and meet in a mating flight over the water. The fertilized females then dip to the surface to *oviposit*, or expel, the eggs that begin the cycle again.

Then both sexes die and fall onto the surface where they are available to the fish again.

Mayflies are represented by fly fishermen during all these stages. We fish nymphs and wet flies to represent the immature forms, floating nymphs to imitate the emerging insects, dun patterns in the form of the classic dry flies, and spinner flies that imitate the spent-wing shape of the dead adults.

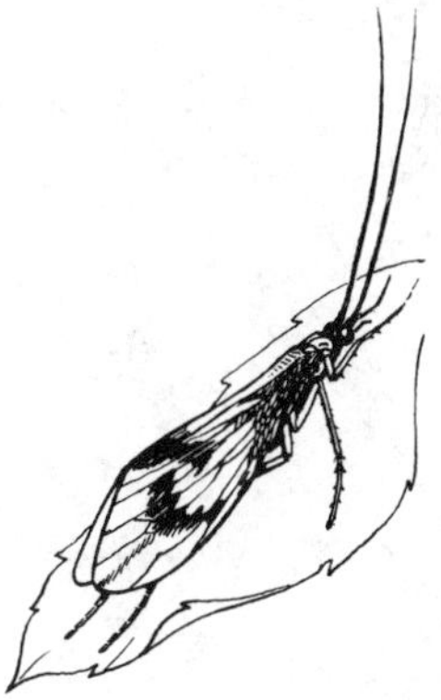

THE CADDISFLIES. Caddisflies have been the subject of greatly expanded interest during the past decade or so not only because they are widely distributed (about eight hundred species in the United States and Canada), but also because they are more tolerant of pollution and warming stream temperatures than mayflies. On many streams, mayfly populations seem to be decreasing while the numbers of caddisflies are holding steady or actually increasing.

Caddisflies are classified in the order *Tricoptera*, a name based on the presence of many tiny hairs on the wings of all species. Unlike mayflies, caddisflies have what entomologists call a "complete" life cycle because they have two underwater stages rather than one. The first stage, called the *larva*, is a worm-like creature that typically builds a case for itself on the bottoms of stream rocks. If you turn over a few rocks in almost any stream that holds fish, you will see caddis cases. Some are made of tiny pebbles and sand grains, some of sticks, some of leaf fragments—all stuck together by a substance secreted by the larva. The various kinds of caddisflies can often be identified by the shape and materials of the case; each genus has a characteristic style of construction. In addition, several "free-living" species do not build cases until the end of the larval stage.

Somewhat before the time of emergence, the larva retreats to the case (the free-living species build a case) and undergoes a process of maturation called *pupation*, as caterpillars do in becoming butterflies. The pupa migrates to the surface, in most species about a year after first being deposited in the stream as an egg.

Pupae shoot to the surface rapidly, often propelled by gas bubbles trapped in the pupal case. The adults are not on the surface long, and they dart around on the surface in preparation for takeoff as soon as they emerge. Some of them literally fly right out of the water. As a result, fish feeding on emerging caddisflies show excited activity, rolling on the surface as they take the pupae and leaping from the water after the escaping adults.

As Figure 6–6 shows, caddisflies are easy to distinguish from mayflies. Their bodies are considerably shorter than their wings, so you will often be deceived into using too-large a fly, and their wings are folded tent-like over their backs at rest. They also fly much differently

Figure 6–5
An adult caddisfly

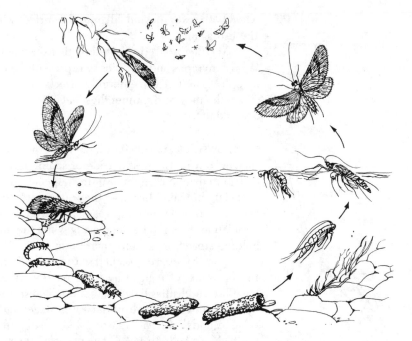

Figure 6–6 The caddisfly life cycle: From the lower left, the larva on the bottom (free-living or case-building) retreats to the case for pupation and emerges as a pupa When the adult emerges from the pupal case, it flies to vegetation and joins the mating swarm. The female oviposits, in this case, underwater.

from mayflies, fluttering rapidly and erratically here and there. Mayflies, by contrast, are often weak fliers, but at least they appear to have a destination in mind!

Caddisflies live longer than mayflies in the adult stage, up to two or three weeks in some species. Mating flights take place in the late afternoon or evening, and in many species the females actually go under the surface and lay their eggs directly on the bottom rubble. Wet flies can be effective imitations of this activity.

Figure 6–7
An adult stonefly

THE STONEFLIES. Stoneflies belong to the order *Plecoptera*, which means "folded wing." Stonefly nymphs prefer fast, rocky streams, and, although they superficially resemble mayfly nymphs, they are easy to distinguish from them. Stonefly nymphs are usually larger, they always have two tails and prominent antennae, and their gills are not along the abdomen but between the legs. Most importantly, stonefly nymphs have a double wing case. Also, stonefly nymphs can be quite large, particularly on Western streams, and they are generally predators, feeding on smaller nymphs and other aquatic organisms.

After a period as a nymph that lasts from one to several years depending on the species, the stonefly nymph emerges by crawling out of the water onto a log or stone. There the winged adult crawls from the nymphal skin. Due to this style of emergence, stoneflies are not usually available to fish during this stage unless high water or winds carry them into the water. Fish may be attracted to the shallows, however, by the migrating nymphs.

In flight the stonefly adult is very clumsy; with all four wings pounding away, it looks very busy indeed. At rest the wings fold flat over the body. During mating swarms and egg-laying, the adults are available to fish and may be taken with greed if there are enough of them to draw the attention of the fish to the surface. On many Western streams the flight of giant stoneflies called "Salmon Flies" can bring huge trout to the surface, inducing hysteria in dry fly fishermen. On Eastern and Midwestern streams stoneflies are most often imitated in the nymph stage, and they are gamefish favorites all year long.

OTHER AQUATIC INSECTS. Several other groups of aquatic insects may be seasonally or locally important. Here's a quick rundown:

Figure 6–8 The stonefly life cycle: From the lower left, the nymph grows larger and emerges onto the streamside rock. The nymph case splits open, and the adult flies away to vegetation. After mating, the females oviposit.

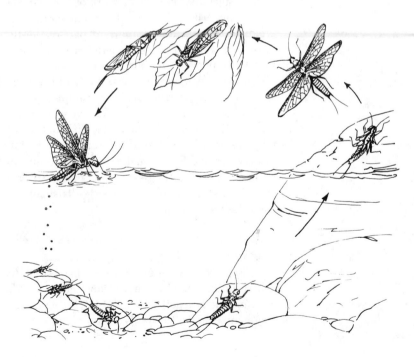

- *Diptera:* This order includes a lot of insects, including the mosquito, but the most important to fly fishermen are the midges. As the order name indicates, midges are two-winged flies. All the others we discussed are four-winged, including the mayflies, although their extra pair of wings are vestigial. Also, most midges are exceedingly small. Present in many streams in enormous numbers, they make up a substantial portion of the food supply. Like the caddisflies, they have a complete life cycle. Most often imitated as pupae and adults, diptera make for sophisticated fishing indeed, requiring tiny flies, light leaders, and a delicate touch.
- *Odonata:* This order includes, among others, the damselflies and dragonflies. Although present in many rivers, these are particularly important food sources in lakes. They are most often represented as nymphs.
- *Megaloptera:* Most important in this group is the dobsonfly, whose larva is popularly known as the "hellgrammite." Smallmouth bass fishermen know this insect as one of the favorite foods of the bass, and trout love them too. Nymph flies, tied to suggest them, can be almost as effective as the real thing.

Terrestrial Insects

Terrestrial insects are land "bugs" that fall or get blown into the water. Since the pioneering work of Vincent Marinaro and Charles K. Fox in the 1940s (more about them in another chapter), imitating these creatures has been an important part of the fly angler's game. Ants, grasshoppers, crickets, and beetles are the major terrestrials, but others may be important on your favorite stream.

Like the aquatic insects, many of the terrestrials are seasonal in their appearance. *Hoppers*, for example, are a late summer insect in most areas, and they are most effective when fished on breezy days when many of the naturals are being blown into the water. Ants are undoubtedly the most versatile of the terrestrial imitations since the natural insect is around for so much of the year. Some anglers who have tasted them—yes, *tasted* them—say ants have a spicy, peppery flavor. Whatever the taste, trout love them and will usually prefer them to other food when they are available.

Crustaceans

Members of this group have a hard shell. Crustaceans are nocturnal, so imitations of them are most effective when fished early in the morning and late in the evening. Of the many varieties, only three are of major importance to the fly fisher.

1. *Scuds* are small, shrimp-like creatures that live in the vegetation found in limestone creeks.
2. *Cress bugs* are found there too.
3. *Crayfish* are the largest of the crustaceans to interest the fly angler, and they are of particular importance to the bass fisherman. Some studies have shown that, where they are numerous, crayfish make up 80 to 90 percent of the diet of smallmouth bass. Trout like them too, so crayfish flies should be in the boxes of anglers who fish waters where they are plentiful.

Forage Fish

Big fish eat little fish. That's why we carry streamers and bucktails. Although some general patterns work well in most waters, becoming familiar with the particular baitfish that inhabit the streams or lakes in your area may be important.

Presentation is important too. Some forage fish, like the sculpin, are exclusively bottom dwellers, while others range throughout the aquatic environment. Knowing the habits and characteristics of the local fish helps you determine the correct presentation and manipulation of the fly.

A Systematic Approach

Even though this discussion of the aquatic environment has been greatly simplified, you can tell by now that fly anglers have a lot of information to keep straight if they are to apply their experience successfully. Most anglers find a fishing log or journal essential for this purpose. Table 6–2 shows a sample page from my fishing journal, but you may wish to model your own from some of the other books I've recommended. My own journal has grown more complicated with the years as I've added more categories, and many anglers would prefer a more simplified system. I find it better, however, to leave some spaces empty than to put too much relevant information in a paragraph at the bottom of the page, where it is more difficult to find and to compare with other pages. Barometric pressure, for example, is a piece of data that I rarely fill in unless I get a local weather forecast that includes it shortly before or after I fish. Still, the category is there when I have the information.

However simple or elaborate you decide to make your journal, be sure that you *do* make one of some type. Our tendency is to trust to memory, but memory does not provide the details that might make a fishing outing successful two or three years from now. Also, our memories are selective. We tend to remember the high points and

Table 6–2 A Page from a Fishing Journal

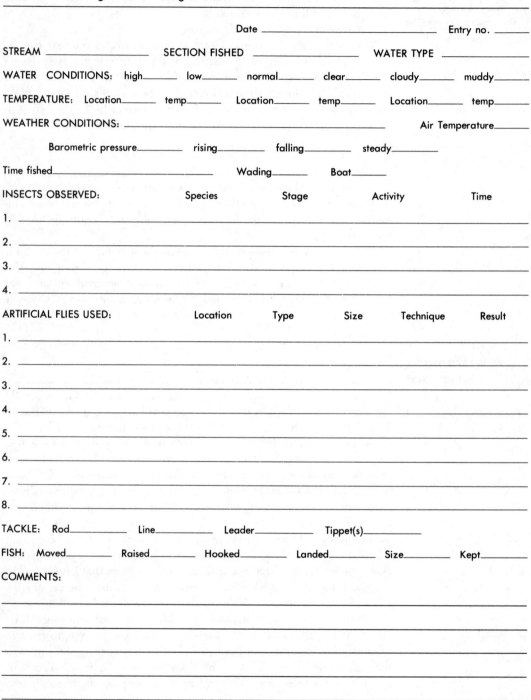

Date _____ Entry no. _____

STREAM _____ SECTION FISHED _____ WATER TYPE _____

WATER CONDITIONS: high_____ low_____ normal_____ clear_____ cloudy_____ muddy_____

TEMPERATURE: Location_____ temp_____ Location_____ temp_____ Location_____ temp_____

WEATHER CONDITIONS: _____ Air Temperature_____

Barometric pressure_____ rising_____ falling_____ steady_____

Time fished_____ Wading_____ Boat_____

INSECTS OBSERVED: Species   Stage   Activity   Time

1. _____

2. _____

3. _____

4. _____

ARTIFICIAL FLIES USED: Location   Type   Size   Technique   Result

1. _____

2. _____

3. _____

4. _____

5. _____

6. _____

7. _____

8. _____

TACKLE: Rod_____ Line_____ Leader_____ Tippet(s)_____

FISH: Moved_____ Raised_____ Hooked_____ Landed_____ Size_____ Kept_____

COMMENTS:

_____

_____

_____

_____

_____

forget the failures, which are often as important to remember as what did work under certain conditions. That's why I include a "result" column for each fly and technique used and ruthlessly enter "zip" when the fish do not respond!

I've organized my journal into a loose-leaf notebook with two major sections, one for bass fishing and one for trout. Within each of these large divisions I have twelve file dividers, one for each month. Then I put all the journal pages for a particular month in one section, arranged sequentially by days. If I have a chance to fish on, say, May 25, I can check and see what worked (and what didn't) on several May 25s in the past, as well as on other days in the same time frame.

Once you have kept a journal for a few years, you begin to see patterns emerging that you would probably not have noted without keeping written records. Certainly you develop a good basis for predicting the emergence of major insects on your local streams, and you usually begin to acquire a sensitivity for the kinds of factors that might bring them on a day or two early one year and delay them for a few days the following year. Most of all, you take on a more modest regard for your own memory as you look over journal entries that describe experiences you no longer recall. That's when you know just how important the journal is.

One final note on fishing journals. If your friends and fishing companions keep one too, you have an ideal basis for comparison. And if you belong to a fishing club, a club journal, to which members contribute entries when they fish local waters, can soon grow into a large body of angling information.

Summing Up

Let me end this chapter by trying to put some of this information into a few general principles that you can begin to make use of immediately. Like all generalizations, these have exceptions, but they might help you to start organizing your knowledge about certain fly fishing situations.

1. Since fish cannot see more than about fifty feet, you can easily get within that range without alarming them as long as you are cautious. If you keep low, move slowly, wear drab clothing, and avoid flashing reflections off your equipment, you can get much closer, especially when approaching from downstream.

2. Feeding fish face the current. So generally they face upstream, except in those few locations where there is a counter-current, such as below a small waterfall or downstream from a large boulder. A fish in such a location might very well be facing downstream, so plan your approach accordingly.

3. If you see fish feeding on a certain insect, attempt to capture one before you tie on a fly and start fishing. If you cannot capture a specimen, rest assured that the real insect is smaller than it appears on the surface or in the air. If it appears from a distance that a #12 fly should match the size of the bug, a #16 will probably be a closer match for the natural.

4. If you capture a specimen of an insect that fish are feeding on but cannot represent all its relevant qualities with any of the flies in your vest, approach the problem in this way: For a surface fly, match the size first, give shape second priority, color third. With a sunken fly, again match size first, but give color second priority and shape third. You can change both the shape and the size of a fly with scissors, and you can darken it with a marking pen. And you can carry a small fly-tying kit in your vest.

5. Study the disturbances that feeding fish make in the water. Just because you see a surface disturbance, don't automatically assume that the fish are taking duns off the surface. That disturbance could be made by their tails as they root for nymphs along the bottom. If you see fish rolling out of the water, showing their dorsal fins like porpoises, they are probably taking emerging nymphs on the way down, not winged adult flies. The rise-form on the water surface produced by a fish taking mayfly duns will show not only spreading rings but also a floating bubble in the middle. The bubble is made by a small amount of air trapped in the roof of the fish's mouth as it comes down over the floating fly. If you see extremely subtle, sipping rises, the kind that sort of "wrinkle" the surface, suspect that the fish are taking spinners, terrestrial insects, or other flush-floating flies (that is, flies that float low and "flush" in the surface film, rather than on top of it). Finally, remember that excited feeding usually means caddisflies or stoneflies. If the fish are jumping out of the water, it is practically certain that a caddis emergence is taking place.

6. When casting to a visible fish, assume that the fish is further from you than it appears and cast accordingly. If you can see the fish itself, remember that refraction makes objects under the surface appear closer than they really are. If you see a rise, remember that by the time the rise rings form they are some distance downstream from where the rise actually took place. Remember also that a rising fish usually allows the current to carry it downstream as it rises toward the surface and then moves back upstream to its original location after taking the fly.

7. Although you will often wish to approach fish from a down-stream direction, note and take advantage of the position of the sun. Fish don't like to look into the sun any more than we do, so if you can get the

sun behind you, you have an advantage. Be careful, however, not to throw a shadow on the water, either your own or that of your rod. And remember that when the sun is at a sharp angle to the surface, the shadow of your floating line might fall over the fish even when the line itself is well away from it.

8. Fish the close water first. Even though you might not see a fish near your location, one might very well be there. If you start off with a cast that "lines" a fish close to you, it is very likely to race upstream in alarm and scatter the fish you might have had a chance to catch. By the same token, when you catch a fish close to your casting location, release it in a direction (usually downstream) that is not likely to alarm the other fish nearby.

9. Careful approaches are almost always more productive than long casts on small streams. Distance casting can be a big asset on a large river or impoundment, but stealth and accuracy pay off on the little waters.

10. Keep the fly in the water. Most fly fishermen, especially beginners, change flies too often. You may have noted that I have only eight listings for flies on my sample journal page. Although I sometimes exceed that number, at least it gently reminds me to fish each fly carefully before changing to another.

11. If the fish aren't on the top, they're on the bottom. Except during a hatch, the intermediate depths in most streams are barren of food. Feeding fish are therefore not likely to be found in this layer of the stream.

12. You'll be more successful if you know something about the habits and behavior of the particular fish that you are seeking. Rainbow trout, for example, prefer faster water than browns, so streams that hold both species will generally contain rainbows in the riffles and browns in the pools. In a given pool, the rainbows should be at the head of the pool, browns at the tail. For another example, smallmouth bass like to hang around rocks, particularly boulders the size of a beer keg and larger. Find such conditions and you should find the fish.

13. Decide to learn something new on every outing. You don't have to catch fish to have a successful trip. If you learn something that you can apply with success in a future situation, then any trip is a success.

Finally, and most important of all, enjoy yourself! If you're not having fun with your fishing, then do it some other way until you do—or drop it altogether and find something that you do enjoy. Fishing isn't a contest, and you don't have to prove anything. If you get your kicks from sticking a few flies in your hatband and fishing them without fuss, more power to you.

You can apply that same selective philosophy to much of what remains in this book. You will probably find that some aspects of fly fishing interest you more than others. So if you want to just skim over the parts that don't interest you now, then feel free to do so. The material will still be here later if you develop an interest.

Recommended Books

Through the Fish's Eye by Mark Sosin and John Clark (Harper & Row, 1973). An outdoor writer and an aquatic biologist team up to give you a view of the fish's world. An excellent introduction to the water world, with emphasis on how the information can be used by anglers.

Comparahatch by Al Caucci and Bob Nastasi (Comparahatch, Ltd., 1973). The first work by this team of angler/entomologists, this is a two-part package. First is a vest-pocket booklet that describes the major mayfly species, complete with information about behavior, size, and emergence times in your area, and with full-color photos of nymphs, duns, spinners, and the flies that represent them, all on waterproof paper. Second is a paperback with more detailed data about each insect, as well as complete tying patterns and instructions for all the flies pictured. Although limited to mayflies, Comparahatch is a great help to the beginner just learning about stream insect life.

7
THE
SUNKEN FLIES:
Wet Flies, Streamers, and Bucktails

The sunken flies—flies that are always fished beneath the surface—are wet flies, bucktails, and streamers. Dry flies, of course, are a "whole different ball game," and nymphs represent a style of fly and a series of fishing techniques that also deserve special attention. I mention the sunken flies first because they are good ones for beginners to use in gaining experience. Although as with other flies, genuine expertise can take years of practice, they are relatively easy to fish successfully, and they require some line and rod manipulation skills that are basic to dry fly and nymph fishing too. If you decide to learn the basic skills with the sunken flies, you'll find yourself well prepared to move on to the other forms of fly fishing.

The Wet Fly

The wet fly is the oldest style of fly. The fly that Aelian saw being fished on the River Astracus in the third century was a wet fly, as were all the subsequent ones until early in the nineteenth century. Obviously, the wet fly is effective, or it could not have lasted for seventeen hundred years. And yet the wet fly is often neglected by modern anglers, who tend to use the more imitative nymphs when they fish underwater.

Today, as in past centuries, there are two basic styles of tying wet flies. The classic wet fly has a "wing" of feather fibers arching back over the hook shank in what is called the *down-wing style*. Another style has no wing but merely soft hackle wrapped as a collar around the front of the fly.

One school of thought sees the wet fly as an "attractor" that stimulates fish to strike by arousing anger, curiosity, or territorial aggression. Those who adhere to this theory usually prefer wet flies in bright colors and flashy tinsel. Another hypothesis is that wet flies work by creating an "impression" of natural life found in the stream, such as insects or small fish. Those who hold this point of view prefer drab flies with colors that run to earth tones like browns, grays, and blacks. And then there are those with a foot in either camp—they fish with two or more flies at a time, often mixing attractors with impressionistic wet flies.

Most of the early flies recommended by the old angling writers were what today we would call the impressionistic types, and many of them are still in use: Flies like the Hare's Ear wet, March Brown, and Blue Dun are examples. Attractor patterns really came into their own on North American waters. The native brook trout that once crowded our streams were not discriminating as far as fly pattern is concerned, and they still aren't. So American fly fishers had great success with bright patterns like the Parmachene Belle, Montreal, and Royal Coachman. In essence, today's wet fly fishing represents the coming together of these two traditions: the drab, somewhat imitative flies of European origin and the flashy wets from the American (and Canadian) past.

Today anglers are more sophisticated and fish more cautious, but the wet fly is still periodically "rediscovered" because it still works,

Figure 7–1 Four classic wet flies: *From the Left:* Royal Coachman, Blue Dun, Dark Hendrickson, and Leadwing Coachman (Photo by Katherine G. Lee)

sometimes when nothing else does. Today, too, authorities have developed new theories to account for the success of the wet fly, some of them based on the growing interest in the caddisflies. It was once thought that a wet fly dragging across the current or being retrieved by the angler could not represent anything natural, but now we know that caddis emergence or egg-laying can be represented by just these techniques.

Fishing the Wet Fly

Of the number of different methods for fishing the wet fly, you will probably use all of them sooner or later. Yet some basic rod-and-line handling techniques are essential in the practice of wet fly fishing, as well as in dry fly and nymph fishing.

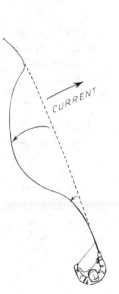

MENDING LINE. When a cast is made across the current, as is often the case in wet fly fishing, the flow of the current between the angler and the fly tends to belly the fly line in a downstream direction, pulling the fly across the current in the process. The result is called *drag* by fly fishermen, and while it is sometimes desirable in wet fly fishing, you need to control it even if you don't want to eliminate it entirely. You can exert this control by "mending" the fly line, that is, by flipping the portion of it that would belly upstream, thereby prolonging the drag-free drift of the fly. (See Figure 7-2.)

Mending is not difficult, especially if you keep your casts short to begin with. By doing so, you will be mending short sections of line initially, and you can go to longer lengths as your skill develops. You will find that a clean, high-floating line mends more easily than a dirty one because it lifts off the surface more cleanly. Even with a sink-tip line, you will often mend the floating portion, so cleaning that portion of the sink-tip is a good idea.

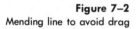

Figure 7-2
Mending line to avoid drag

As you become an accomplished caster you may learn to mend the line while the cast is still in the air. Just before the line loop turns over, make the same little upstream flip that you make if the line is already on the water. The line should fall with an upstream belly already there.

In wet fly and streamer fishing, where the cast is often made across the current, you have to mend the line often. Here is another case when a long rod is advantageous; you can mend a longer line more easily with a long rod.

RETRIEVING LINE. In most forms of fly fishing, wet fly fishing included, you need to retrieve line, either as a way of manipulating the fly or as a method of taking up slack line as the fly drifts toward you after an upstream cast. You may use several different retrieves. For each of them you need secure control of the line, so you can clamp down and set the hook if a fish should strike at any point during the drift of the fly or the retrieve itself.

The key to this control is shown in Figure 7–3. Note that the line is controlled at all times by the middle finger of the rod hand. Some prefer to use the first finger; take your choice. Even when the finger is relaxed the line is under control. If a fish hits, the line finger can tighten immediately, eliminating the slack that would otherwise occur. You should use this line control method at all times, except when you're using one of the line-hand retrieves (discussed shortly). Fly fishing is just like other types of fishing in this respect: you can't hook fish effectively unless your line is under control.

Retrieving the fly can take several forms. The simplest is the *strip retrieve*, in which the line hand strips in the line in a series of pulls, often interspersed with pauses. The line strips can be long or short, slow or fast, but in between strips the line control finger must close on the line while the retrieving hand reaches for another strip. The line retrieved by the strip can be collected in coils or simply dropped on the water.

Another popular retrieve is the *hand-twist retrieve*. Unlike the strip retrieve, the hand-twist produces a steady, regular motion in the fly, and it lends itself to many speed variations.

I prefer the *line-weaving technique* developed by Leon Chandler. A few years ago I attended a Brotherhood of the Jungle Cock Campfire (more about the Brotherhood later) at which Leon, as a special guest, put on a fine casting demonstration for the youngsters. As he retrieved line, even during false casting, he "knitted" the line on his fingers and then shot it off again as he made another cast. After the demonstration, Leon showed me how he does it, and I have been using his method ever since.

Like many fly fishing skills, the line-weave looks complicated, but with a little practice it becomes a natural motion that begins to occur

Figure 7–3 The line control finger (Photo by Katherine G. Lee)

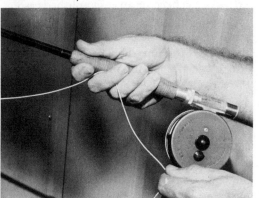

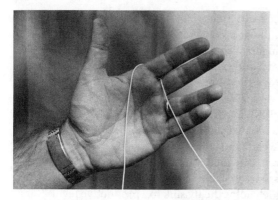

1. Over the first finger.

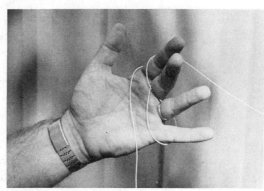

2. Around three and in between two.

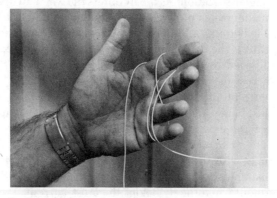

3. Over the first to begin the sequence again.

Figure 7–4 The Leon Chandler line-weave.

automatically. The series of pictures that make up Figure 7–4 will help to make the action clear. The line goes over the first finger, around the remaining three, and then between the two middle fingers. The sequence again: Over one, around three, between two. This action produces a figure-eight configuration with one end around the first finger and the other around the last two, with the middle finger providing the guidance and separating the two loops of the figure eight.

This technique is superior to the hand-twist retrieve for a number of reasons. First, it is less destructive to fly line because it does not bend the line into such tight loops as the hand-twist. Tight bends in a fly line can lead to cracking of the finish (and, as Vice President of the Cortland Line Company, Leon Chandler knows a thing or two about fly line care). Also, the line-weave provides more control than the hand-twist, and, since the line is woven around the fingers, the snarls that sometimes develop with the hand-twist are eliminated. Finally, the line weave allows much greater speed variations than the hand-twist. Either bringing in the line quite rapidly or a slow crawl is easy. Although the line is stored securely on the fingers it shoots off readily when the cast is made. I think the line-weave is far and away the best method of retrieve when a slow or steady retrieve is called for.

THE CLASSIC WET FLY TECHNIQUE. Once you can mend and retrieve line, you are ready for the classic method of fishing the wet fly. This method calls for an across-the-stream-and-down delivery of the fly, with the fly swinging across the current at a point below the angler. The beginning of the sequence is an across-stream cast. It might be a little upstream from the angler's position, which helps the fly sink to a productive level. But it might also be directly across the current or a little downstream from the angler's location. As the fly enters the water an upstream mend is usually made, which prolongs the drift of the fly and also helps it to sink close to the bottom. Additional mends may be made as necessary to prolong the drift of the fly. When the fly reaches the intended target area, the line is allowed to tighten and to belly slightly downstream, pulling the fly across the current and toward the surface. The fly continues across the current until it is directly below the angler, at which time it is usually just below the surface. Then the fly is retrieved until the pickup is made for the next cast.

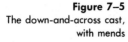

Figure 7–5
The down-and-across cast, with mends

You may fish the fly in this way without additional motion, or you may wish to throw in rod tip twitches, short line strips, or any other manipulation that you hope will trigger strikes. Strikes are most frequent when the fly begins the cross-current "swing" below the angler. Since the fly also begins to rise from the bottom at this point, it represents some of the behavior of an emerging insect. Strikes may also occur when the fly is hanging directly downstream, and many wet fly fishermen like to prolong this portion of the technique with jiggles of the rod tip and slow withdrawals of the fly, accompanied by slack-line drifts back to the original position. Finally, the fly is sometimes taken while drifting freely before the fly swing begins, so you must watch the end of the line carefully—you will probably not feel such a strike.

You can prolong the drift of the fly at any point by feeding additional slack line into the drift. Even when the fly is drifting freely, you can add additional line by stripping it off the reel and feeding it through the guides while "shivering" the rod back and forth, in a somewhat slower version of the motion that you use in the snake cast. Conversely, the drift of the fly can be checked at any point by clamping down with the line control finger; this tightens the line, and the cross-current swing begins.

When you use this wet fly technique, be sure that you fish the water systematically. Make your first cast swing into the beginning of what you expect to be productive water, and make sure that you probe

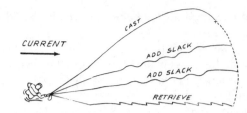

Figure 7–6 Adding slack to prolong the drift

each likely area carefully. On the other hand, there's no use casting repeatedly into the same area with a wet fly; if a fish is going to strike the fly, it will probably do so on the first cast or two. To combine thoroughness and efficiency, many wet fly fishermen make several casts and then step downstream one or two paces, make a few more casts, step downstream again, and so on.

Sometimes you see fish swirl at the fly, or even bump it, without actually striking seriously. If this happens when using a bright fly, try changing to a somber pattern—the fish often takes it on the first cast. If you are already using a somber pattern, try a smaller size or switch to another dark fly.

THE MULTI-FLY CAST. Most wet fly fishermen use a multi-fly cast at least occasionally. It's a good way to cover all the bases when you don't really know a stretch of water well or don't know what sort of insect activity to expect. Most wet fly fishing is "prospecting" anyway, in the sense that you can't see the fish or know exactly what they are doing. So the multi-fly cast allows you to hedge your bets a little.

You need to use blood knots in a leader for fishing more than one fly. If you start with only two flies, you won't have so many problems. Tie on the tippet, making sure that the pre-tippet strand is much longer than usual, and tie the blood knot so that about eight to ten inches of that strand are left standing out on one side of the knot. Then just clip the

Figure 7–7 A two-fly leader

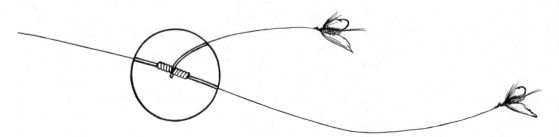

other side of the knot close and you have a "dropper" for attaching your second fly.

Note that the "waste" that you want to use for the dropper is not from the tippet material, but from the next-heavier strand of the leader. A dropper should stand out stiffly from the rest of the leader to minimize tangles, and the heavier strand in a blood knot stands out more stiffly from the knot than the lighter strand. The tippet, to which the point fly is attached, should be eighteen to twenty inches long. This length keeps the two flies separated enough to make tangles less frequent, and the two flies cover more water.

If you want to fish more than one fly on a regular basis, you should make up some special leaders for such fishing. Ideally, a multi-fly leader should be made entirely of stiff monofilament to keep the flies separated; the soft, supple nylon previously recommended for tippets isn't so good. If you want to fish more than two flies, add the additional ones the same way you added the first, always using the stiffer (larger) of the two mono sections for the dropper.

When fishing two flies (I never fish more), I like to mix one attractor and one more subtle pattern, so I usually fish a Royal Coachman on one strand and a Dark Cahill on the other. Usually, each of the flies gets some attention. But if I find I'm getting all my strikes on one fly or the other, I change the second fly for another of the one that's getting all the action. Occasionally I can get a "double," especially when fishing for smallmouth bass. When one of these very competitive fish takes the fly, another often goes over to try to steal it, sees the second fly, and gets hooked too. So far I've never had this happen with large fish, but, if you fish more than one fly, be prepared for the possibility of more than one fish at a time!

Casting two flies isn't difficult if the leader is built properly. Slowing down the casting stroke a little usually helps, and this is one situation where a wide loop is more desirable than a tight one. If you want a wider line loop than usual, move the rod tip through a wider-than-usual arc. But don't try for distance with a multi-fly cast. You'll tangle the leader or mess up your casting stroke or both. If you want to fish three flies or more, more power to you, but you're on your own!

OTHER WET FLY TECHNIQUES. In addition to the classic across-and-down presentation, wet flies can be fished upstream. In this procedure, short, accurate casts are used to place the fly far enough upstream of a likely holding area that it sinks to a productive level and drifts freely back downstream toward the angler. The technique is a lot like "prospecting" with the dry fly (which we'll examine more fully in the next chapter). Since the fly is drifting back toward the angler, the line must be retrieved with the line hand in order to take up slack and allow for a successful hookup should a fish take the fly. The line may be finger-woven with the line hand, if the current is slow, or stripped in, if the flow is faster.

The "take" of an upstream wet fly can be extremely subtle, and experienced fishermen look for their lines or leaders to twitch or hesitate in their downstream float. If the water is clear and shallow, you may see a fish move to the fly or see a flash of a turning belly under water. If so, strike by lifting the rod. If you've kept the slack under control, you should be connected. Most beginners miss a few fish before they get the hang of striking properly, especially when fishing upstream. Setting the hook is much easier with the downstream presentation: A fish often hooks itself on the strike; at least most of the strikes are obvious, so you can rapidly learn to respond correctly to them. The upstream technique is more difficult since you usually don't feel the fish until after you have set the hook. The rule here is, if in doubt, strike! You'll hook the bottom many times, of course, but you'll hook a lot of fish too.

You will also find it useful to try wet flies during hatches, particularly caddis emergences. Many of the classic wet flies of a somber tone, like the Hare's Ear and the Leadwing Coachman, are good imitations of caddis pupae. And a fairly fast line-weave retrieve is a good representation of the motions of emerging pupae. Don't forget that egg-laying caddis females are also well represented by wet flies; again, the earth-toned patterns are best. Even in mayfly hatches, wet flies can be effective. Members of the Iron genus leave their nymphal shucks on the bottom and migrate to the surface with their wings already exposed. And even though most other mayflies emerge on the surface, some of the emergers get stuck in the nymph case and drift along just under the surface with their wings half out of the shuck. The typical wet fly pattern represents this so-called *stillborn* very well.

No wonder, then, that wet flies keep getting "rediscovered." Although they may not often be exact imitations of underwater forms, they are powerfully suggestive under a host of different circumstances. Fly fishermen have caught fish with wet flies for two thousand years. You will too.

Streamers and Bucktails

Streamers and bucktails, as you know, imitate small fish that bigger fish feed on. Streamers are tied with feathers, bucktails with animal hair. Most of the early streamers were elongated versions of successful wet fly patterns; in fact, it seems certain that fish take some wet flies for little minnows or dace. If you watch a wet fly in the water, you quickly see what the inventors of the streamer must have seen—that a slightly elongated body and wing might make the deception even more successful.

While some streamers still reflect gaudy wet fly origins, many others have been designed around the same suggestive philosophy that led to the development of the subdued wet fly patterns. While many stream fish show a flash of silver from their scales, their primary colors (except perhaps during the spawning season) are more somber: browns, olives, blacks. Many of the most successful of the modern minnow-flies reflect this fact.

The feather-wing streamer has a number of advantages from the standpoint of imitation. The feather wing, if properly tied from soft hackle, seems to "breathe" as it undulates through the water. Unfortunately, it also tends to foul around the hook bend after a few casts. A recent trend, also based on a rediscovery of an ancient practice, is the *matuka* style of streamer, in which the wing is lashed down all along the top of the hook, usually with tinsel or fine wire. As you can see in Figure 7–8, the matuka style solves the problem of the errant wing while preserving the attraction of the feather fly.

Bucktail flies do not have the same breathing action as the streamers but they are just as effective. Probably they work by presenting a realistic profile to the predator fish. The Muddler Minnow, undoubtedly the all-time favorite minnow-fly, doesn't look much like a baitfish on the tying bench, but it sure does catch fish in the water. The Muddler, as Figure 7–9 shows, has a shaggy head of clipped deer hair, as well as a combination feather and bucktail wing. The feather in this case does not provide much action but contributes to the profile that seems so critical to the success of the fly. Many anglers believe that the deer hair head pushing through the water is also one of the secrets of the fly's effectiveness. Whatever the reason, if you turned the average fly fisherman loose with the restriction that he could fish only one fly, it would probably be the Muddler.

Another variation of the streamer theme is the marabou fly.

Figure 7–8 *Top:* A standard-tie badger streamer. *Bottom:* The Matuka version. (Photo by Katherine G. Lee)

Figure 7–9 The deadly Muddler Minnow (Photo by Katherine G. Lee)

Marabou is a name given to the soft, fluffy feathers found close to the skin of some birds. Marabou undulates and pulsates when manipulated in the water, streamlining when pulled and billowing out again when stopped, providing a life-like swimming action that is deadly attractive to game fish. Marabou is often incorporated into a number of standard flies to make them more effective under certain conditions. The Marabou Muddler is one example.

Fishing the Streamer

The standard streamer and bucktail technique is based on the classic wet fly approach. The angler casts the fly across the current, mends the line, and follows the fly swing intently. After the swing is completed, the fly is retrieved, usually with the line strip technique. There are many variations on this basic theme, but, as with the wet fly, many of the strikes come as the fly swings across the current.

Just as in wet fly fishing, mending line is an important skill in streamer and bucktail fishing. With the cross-stream cast, upstream mends aid in sinking the fly, and downstream mends swim the fly broadside to the flow. You might need to make both types of mends on a single cast: first upstream to sink the fly, and then downstream to swim the fly right past a promising spot.

On small streams, a streamer or bucktail can often be poked into suspected lies, allowed to sink, and then jiggled up and down. This approach can be a most effective technique with flies tied from high-action materials like marabou. Also, it is often effective to let a streamer drift downstream on a slack line, fluttering the fly to life as it reaches an area where you suspect there is a fish.

Most anglers feel that streamers and bucktails are most effective when they seem to duplicate the odd behavior of a baitfish that is sick or injured. It is well known that predators are attracted to any prey that seems especially vulnerable; this is one way in which the weak and poorly adapted are eliminated. Many observations have shown that the predator fish often remain close to schools of potential prey without attacking until they spot an individual that behaves strangely. That individual triggers the attack, which may then spread to the rest of the school. As many of the baitfish in the school are injured by the attack, the feeding builds to a fury of violence until the predator fish are satiated.

How can you represent an injured or sick baitfish? Just about anything you do may work. In fact, it would probably be impossible for you to manipulate your fly so that it would swim like a normal, healthy minnow, so anything you do to impart action to the fly probably looks unhealthy. This is one of the reasons why streamers and bucktails are good flies for beginners to use.

Nevertheless, some techniques work better than others on a given day, so be prepared to experiment with the speed and style of your retrieve. Sometimes the strip retrieve is the one that works, but other times you need a retrieve so slow that the line-weave is called for. I even find a dead-drift presentation, with no imparted motion at all, frequently effective. Be systematic in your experimentation, and keep trying until you hit on the combination that works at that particular time.

I've found it useful to base the motion of my fly on what I know about the fish that are present. A sculpin, for example, is a poor swimmer. So when I fish an imitation of this fish, I try to creep it along the bottom with an occasional weak spurt thrown in. A crayfish scurries about when alarmed, so I crawl the fly for a while and scoot it a few inches. You will benefit by learning about the natural behavior of the organisms that your streamers and bucktails represent. Even though you want an injured or crippled-looking action, it must still resemble the behavior of a natural fish.

SINKING THE FLY. One of the major problems in streamer fishing is getting the fly down to where the fish are. Many of these patterns have to be fished right on the bottom to be effective, a sometimes difficult task in waters of substantial depth. Current speed plays a role too. Getting a fly to the bottom and making it stay there in a rapidly flowing stream can be extremely difficult. The current carries the fly downstream until the line tightens, and then the fly comes back up again.

The obvious way to sink the fly, of course, is to weight the fly, the leader, or both with lead. The problem with this option is that it makes casting unpleasant and detracts from the action of the fly. Nevertheless, lead must often be used. I try to limit the amount used as much as possible. Here are some suggestions:

1. *Tie the fly with absorbent materials.* You might be surprised how many streamers and bucktails are tied with materials that actually

float. The Muddler Minnow, for example, incorporates a deer hair head, and the floating tendency of the hollow deer hair has to be overcome before the fly will sink. Now I'm a big fan of the Muddler, but when I tie one for deep fishing I either trim the head down very small or eliminate the deer hair altogether. I've found that an effective Muddler can be made with a head of spun rabbit fur, clipped to the same shaggy profile as the standard deer hair head. I've used this variation for about eight years now, and the other anglers I've persuaded to try it have reported favorable results too.

2. *Weight the fly in the tying process.* Many commercially available streamers are weighted, and you might want to weight yours when you get into tying flies. I used to weight mine heavily, but now I try to work for a more neutral buoyancy, so I add only enough lead to offset the buoyancy of the materials used in tying the fly. Then, if necessary, I can always add more weight to the leader.

3. *Use a sinking solution.* This stuff was recommended back in the accessories section. It doesn't make the fly heavier, but it speeds up the saturation process so that the fly is fully soaked after the first cast or so, rather than after the first ten minutes. Consequently, you can get by with less weight to start with.

Figure 7–10 The Shenk Sculpin. This one is shown in a fly tying vise made by Eric Price of Price's Angler's Corner. (Photo by Katherine G. Lee)

4. *Saturate the fly before the first cast,* if you don't use the sink solution. Many streamers and bucktails are made of materials that absorb water, but only gradually. If you put the fly underwater and squeeze it before making the first cast, it gets down where you want it a lot easier.

5. *Use sinking lines when necessary.* There is no doubt that a floating line is easier and more pleasant to fish than a sinking one, but many anglers try to stretch the capabilities of the floating line beyond its limits. Where strong currents and waist-deep depths meet, I go to a sink-tip line with a short leader. The floating section can be mended when necessary, and, with the new fluorescent sink sections now available, the location and progress of the fly can be followed much more easily. I think the sink-tip line is a more desirable alternative than adding gobs of lead, at least in streamer fishing.

6. *When all else fails, add more lead.* I like to add it in small increments, so that I can quit without overdoing it. You'll need several sizes of shot for small stream work, especially since you are not likely to use the sinking line option there. I like the small packs of micro-shot as well as the larger removable shot.

Casting Weighted Streamers

Casting a heavily weighted streamer is no picnic. Fly rods and lines, as you know, are designed for casting nearly weightless lures, so when you start adding weight to flies you move into an area where the principles of fly casting and those of bait casting collide. The results are not esthetically pleasing, and they can be dangerous. Many a weighted streamer has found its way into an angler's shoulder or ear.

Most casters tend to speed up their casting stroke when fishing with weighted flies, when slowing down would work better. When you're a little afraid of being hit with the darn thing, it seems natural to hurry up and heave it out there. But by slowing your stroke and opening your loop a little, the cast can be made more safely.

Another bad habit of some casters when using these flies is overpowering the forward stroke and driving the rod tip down parallel with the water. Again, this is a natural tendency. You're afraid the heavy streamer will collide with your nice rod, so you push the rod out of the way. But soon you're only slinging the fly, not casting it, and ultimately this tendency may develop into a habit and ruin your regular casting stroke.

Actually, you'll make a better cast with a weighted streamer if you stop the rod high on the forward stroke and let the line loop form as it should. That way you get the weight of the line working in the cast, along with the weight of the fly. If you remember this principle, perhaps you can avoid the bad habits that casting weighted flies can develop.

Ultimately, expert casters are not so much those who can cast all the line off the reel, but those who can put the fly anywhere they want it. I got an object lesson in this truth once when I had the privilege of fishing with Ed Shenk of Carlisle, Pennsylvania. Ed has the reputation of being one of the premier fly anglers in the country, and, after seeing him in action, I know why. We started our morning on the Letort Spring Run by fishing with the Shenk Sculpin, one of a number of now standard flies that Ed originated. He fishes the sculpin with a shot the size of your little fingernail, right in front of the knot, so that it will sink immediately to the bottom upon hitting the water. Casting only the leader and two or three feet of line, Ed repeatedly dropped the big streamer exactly where he wanted it.

I fish the sculpin a lot myself but never exactly like this. I'd never weighted the fly so heavily, and I was used to making much longer casts in which the line helped to carry the fly to the target. Under these new conditions I had no idea where the fly was going, although I suspected that my hair was one likely destination. When I did manage to hit the water, it sounded like someone had thrown a brick in. Ed's soft lob landed with a quiet "plop."

After I demonstrated my inadequacy with the sculpin for a couple of hours, we reached a point where the stream flowed under a local road. The bridge was only a foot or so above the flow, and so low you had to bend over to look under it.

"Try an ant under the bridge," said Ed. "You won't be able to see the fish take it, so listen." With some trepidation I pieced my leader out to 6X, tied on the #16 ant, and tried to cast it up under the bridge. I hit the bridge with a few casts and the water with a few more. A couple of the casts landed a little way under the bridge.

Sure enough, I heard the trout. I set the hook too hard and broke off a fish of good size.

Then Ed had his turn. After all morning of lobbing that big sculpin around, he tied on an ant on 6X and proceeded to zing about twenty straight casts under the bridge. Some of them went so far under that it's a wonder the ant didn't come out the other side.

Ed raised a trout too, another heavy one, but the fish broke off on the strike just as mine had. But what a casting demonstration—and not the sort you see at the sportsman's shows!

The Shenk Sculpin is one fly that must be fished right on the bottom, and there are others. If you intend to fish them (and to have a chance at the big fish they attract), you have to practice some unorthodox methods. But be sure you don't alter your basic casting style in the process.

As usual, this chapter concludes with a couple of books that can expand your understanding of fishing with wet flies and streamers. In addition, the Appendix contains a list of the dressings for the flies I've described, in case you want to try them in some of the situations we've discussed. Most of these flies can be ordered through catalogs or bought at fly shops. The patterns are for your convenience if you want to tie your own (and I hope you will), or you can order custom-tied flies from a tier in your area.

There are, of course, many other wet flies and streamers besides those we've discussed, but these few should serve you well to get started. And once you've started, you'll find out what suits you and your conditions best. You can take it from there!

Recommended Books

The Soft-Hackled Fly by Sylvester Nemes (Chatham Press, 1975). One of the most recent books to recognize the value of the wet fly and one that offers some unique approaches to insect imitation using the sunken fly. Nemes sees the wet fly as an imitative fly, and his recommendations for tying successful wets have proved highly useful.

Streamers and Bucktails: The Big Fish Flies by Joseph D. Bates, Jr. (Alfred A. Knopf, Inc., 1980). The definitive book on streamer fishing, recently out in a new and updated edition. Lots of photos, color plates, fly patterns, and fishing tips. Essential for the streamer fisherman.

8
SURFACE
FLIES:
Dry Flies and Bass Bugs

One of the most enjoyable sights in fly fishing is the rise of a fish to a floating fly. It may be a savage swirl or a subtle sip. It may come unexpectedly or only after long observation and patient fly selection. But when it comes, and when you raise the rod and feel the throbbing weight of a good fish on the other end, nothing in fly fishing is more exciting.

Certainly that satisfaction—of actually seeing the response of a fish to the cast—was one of the basic elements in the rapid rise to popularity of dry fly fishing in the nineteenth century. Certainly, too, the free rising trout of the rich limestone creeks of England played an important part. Had dry fly fishing had its origins on a rushing freestone stream in America, many of the traditions (and dogmas) attached to this aspect of fly fishing might never have developed.

Frederick Halford is the father of dry fly fishing, or at least its major popularizer. Halford advocated the upstream cast, the freely drifting fly, and the careful imitation of a natural insect on which the fish was already feeding. While these techniques certainly have their place on American waters, today's anglers also recognize the need for *prospecting*, or "fishing the water," when no feeding fish are seen. And, if the truth be known, many modern fly flingers cast their dry flies down-stream occasionally, and a few actually twitch their floating flies!

American fly fishermen also pioneered the use of surface flies for fish other than trout. Bass bugging for largemouth and smallmouth bass is a specialized art in itself, and the floating fly is also sometimes used in saltwater fly rodding. So the surface fly has come to have a role far beyond that first assigned to it on the chalk streams of England.

Dry fly fishing can be an ideal form of fly fishing for the beginner. Contrary to what many people believe, dry fly fishing is not particularly difficult. Moreover, since the fly can be seen on the water, not only can beginners see how to make a cast to put the fly in a particular location, but they can also rapidly learn the consequences of "drag" and how it can be avoided. Most important, they can have the powerful reward of seeing fish rise to, and get hooked on, their flies. Once you have some experience with the dry fly, you will be more skillful with sunken flies too, because you will be better able to judge the location of the fly and how it is behaving even though you can't see it. For all these reasons, don't shrink from the dry fly. If it interests you, get right into it.

As we did for wet flies and streamers, let's discuss some techniques for fishing the floating fly, describe some common situations in which a floater might be successful, and recommend a few patterns. First to be considered, however, are some of the principles involved in presenting a surface fly to a fish.

The "Window" Phenomenon

When a fish looks up at the surface of the water, most of what it sees is a reflection of the bottom of the stream. In this "mirror," surface objects are visible only to the extent that they protrude either under the surface or into the surface film, which is called the *meniscus,* and which is created by the surface tension of the water. Extremely light objects, such as insects, may not protrude through the film, but they do press it down a little, creating a series of "wrinkles" that the fish sees as a pattern of light.

The only place where the fish can see out *through* the surface is at the *window,* a conical field of view with its circular base at the surface of the water and its point at the fish's eye. The window is a product of the principle of refraction; light rays are bent as they enter water, as you will remember if you've ever seen the old demonstration of a pencil in a glass of water. Strictly speaking, the fish can see *everything* that is above the surface, but the objects at the edge of the window are sharply com-pressed and blurred. Only those objects near the center of the window are clear and distinct.

The size of the window is a function of the fish's depth below the

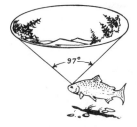

Above: The window is a cone with its point at the fish's eye. (The fish is shown in profile for clarity.)
Below: The dry fly floats toward the feed area. Inside each oval is what the fish see in the window.

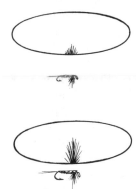

Figure 8–1
The window phenomenon

surface: the deeper the fish, the larger the window. Fish actively feeding at the surface, however, generally hold at a shallow depth so that they don't have to rise so far to take a floating insect. Thus the window of a surface-feeding fish is usually small, and the portion that offers sharp definition is still smaller.

Naturally, the window moves with the fish. As the fish moves, objects on the surface may come into the window clearly and then become indistinct blurs at the edges again. In a stream the surface itself is moving, so a floating object may come into clear view and then move away again even when the fish is stationary. Thus all these factors enter into the fish's vision on the surface: the depth of the fish, the movement of the fish, and the speed of the current, along with, of course, the clarity of the water and the amount of light available.

Why does all this matter to the angler fishing a surface fly? Simply because the floating fly has to get into the window to be taken by the fish. A lake fisherman, for example, often faces the problem of *cruising* fish. These fish move around while feeding, taking their windows with them. The angler's problem is to anticipate where the fish will go next and place the fly so that it has a chance to appear in the window. Stream fishermen face a different situation. The fish is usually holding in one small area, so they use the current to carry their flies into the window, just as it carries the natural insects that the fish feeds on.

Because of the peculiar things that bent light rays do to visual objects, you may be surprised at how the fish sees a floating fly. Imagine a fish facing upstream in current, looking up in anticipation of a natural insect. Here is what the fish sees as the fly drifts toward it: The first things seen are the hackles, tails, and perhaps the bend and point of the hook, pressing down into or through the mirrored surface just as might the feet and abdomen of a natural insect. All of this is visible before the fly gets into the window. As the fly approaches the edge of the window, the first thing to come into the fish's view is whatever is *highest* on the fly (not what is in front, necessarily), such as the wing or the top of the hackle. This material at the top of the fly appears alone, separated by some distance from the portion still projecting through the surface. Finally, as the fly moves into the distinct center of the window, the top of the fly and the bottom come together and the fly is seen as a single entity. Check Figure 8–1 for a visual representation of this phenomenon.

With the complexities of underwater vision, it's no wonder that experts differ on how to design flies to imitate natural insects on the surface. Some think it best to concentrate on the bottom features of the fly, particularly the hackle collar, tails, and body. Their reasoning is that these portions project into the surface like the feet and abdomen of the natural insect and that they are usually the first elements of the fly to capture the attention of the fish. Others insist that the wing is most important because, as the highest part of the fly, it is the first portion to actually appear in the window. Some say that omitting the hackle entirely is best because it only obscures the essential wing. Others omit wings and tie all-hackle flies. Undoubtedly all the factions are correct, but not at the same time. Just about any sort of dry fly will catch fish, but some types are better than others in particular situations. And the window phenomenon is usually the underlying cause.

Getting Started with the Dry Fly

I recommend that you start fishing the dry fly in fast water. Riffle areas of trout streams are often neglected by beginners and experienced anglers alike. The majority of fly fishermen, for some reason, head for the pools and leave the fast water to those who know how productive it can be.

Fishing the fast-water sections of a stream offers a number of advantages to the angler. First, the fish holding in such water are likely to be receptive to anything that looks edible. If they weren't interested in feeding, they probably wouldn't be in the stressful currents of the riffle areas. A fish in such water is usually an "opportunistic" feeder, willing to settle for anything that looks "buggy" rather than insisting on a particular morsel. Also, a fish in fast water has very little time to scrutinize a fly. The current is carrying it rapidly away, and the fish that hesitates misses an opportunity to feed. An added advantage of the fast water is that the broken surface of the riffles makes the fish less likely to observe the angler's approach and renders the choice of tippet size less critical than it would be in a quiet-water section. Fly selection isn't critical, either; with a fast-water fly, good flotation and visibility to the angler are more important than precise imitation.

The problem in fast-water dry fly fishing is the same as in other locations: drag. As you know, drag occurs when the current pulls on the line or leader, causing the fly to cross the current in an unnatural manner or to float faster or more slowly than other objects in the same line of drift. When your fly is seen and rejected by a fast-water fish, drag is almost always responsible. So here's yet another advantage of fast-water dry fly angling: you learn about drag rapidly because you see it on the water and you see the result.

Two casting skills are at a premium in fishing the dry fly in riffle areas: accuracy and the ability to throw a slack line. Most of the casts are short, and, indeed, you often fish only the leader and a couple of feet of line. So you need to achieve pin-point accuracy with short casts. On longer casts, you need to throw some slack into the line, perhaps with the snake cast, so that you can get a few feet of drag-free float before the current whisks the fly away. If you can make these casts and put the fly in a fish's location, the chances are high that it will rise to your fly.

Knowing what you do about the effects of current stress on fish,

Figure 8–2
The snake cast

you will probably be surprised at all the fish you raise in the riffles. They are there because they have found locations for feeding lies that are less stressful than the overall current. Learn to look for any "pocket" of water that seems even slightly less rapid than the surrounding currents. Such a pocket might be in the eddy of a stream boulder. It might be at the foot of a miniature falls or where the tail of a pool begins down over a riffle. It might be a depression on the bottom, where additional depth provides a fish with current relief. Look also for those areas that probably harbor fish even though the surface currents appear swift. A rock creates an area of reduced pressure upstream as well as down, and the area may be large enough to hold a fish. The sides of large rocks are also good places to drift a dry fly along because a fish often holds along the edge of a rock to one side or the other. These fish-holding pockets need not be large. Any area of reduced current pressure the size of a bushel basket might hold a fish of good size.

In spite of your best efforts, your fly will often drag through a particularly promising piece of water. Don't despair, just keep trying until you get a good float through the area. While it's true that your first cast is the most likely one to succeed, feeding fish in fast water are not too likely to be *put down* (frightened enough to stop feeding) by a dragging fly unless it drags just as they attempt to take it. Even then you might raise the fish again after resting that section for a while or changing to another fly pattern. Even if you alarm a fish in one pocket, it will probably flee downstream if it has a clear avenue of escape that doesn't include running into you. This is another reason to avoid wading when possible: You give the fish a downstream escape route so they leave the fish upstream unalerted to your presence. In this sort of *pocket prospecting*, you can make a lot of mistakes and still catch fish.

Remember that visibility and flotation are critical in a fast-water fly. As regards visibility, if you can't see the fly, you can't tell if you have achieved a good float over a certain section. And you will miss strikes if you can't tell whether a rise is to your fly or to some natural food item. And as regards flotation, if a fly won't float after being bounced around a bit, it won't be a good performer in this type of fishing. On small creeks I like the *bi-visible* style of fly, an all-hackle fly in which most of the hackle is a somber color with one or two turns of white hackle added at the head of the fly for visibility. For fishing in heavy water, such as that often found in the West, heavily hackled dries (the Wulff series, for instance), or the deer-hair bodied flies (such as the Humpy) are both good. These flies float like corks; they can be drowned by a crashing waterfall and come back for more. There is little reason to change flies often in fast-water fishing—at least the fish don't require it—so you don't want to be changing continuously just because your flies won't float.

False casting, of course, is necessary to dry the fly between floats. But don't overdo it. A lot of anglers seem to get mesmerized by the act of casting; they keep flicking the fly back and forth in the air. You can occasionally catch a bird that way, but the fish are few and far between. False cast the water off the fly, and then get it back on the water.

Tippet size should be governed by the water and by the size of fish you expect to find there. On the Eastern mountain streams that I fish most often, I use 5X most of the time and then 6X during the low water of late summer and fall. I suppose a few fish break off with these light tippets that I might land with heavier nylon, but I raise a lot more. So I think I come out ahead.

Although most of your fishing in this fast-water prospecting will be upstream, don't overlook the possibility of a downstream presentation. If you can't get the fly to a fish without a drag, then try drifting the fly down to its location on a slack line. And if caddisflies are emerging, the downstream presentation of the dry fly allows you to twitch the fly in an upstream direction, only an inch or so, representing the behavior of the natural insect. This can be a devastating technique at such times. Remember that you need an especially cautious approach to get into position for a downstream cast.

Other Dry Fly Tactics

Basically, dry fly fishing for trout can be reduced to two essential tactics:

1. *fishing the water* (or prospecting), which involves casting a dry fly into likely locations or to fish you have spotted but have not seen take a particular insect; and
2. *fishing the rise* (also called "matching the hatch"), in which you attempt to imitate a particular insect that a fish has taken.

Sometimes the difference between these two approaches is not clear-cut.

Fishing the Water

ON FREESTONE STREAMS. Prospecting with a dry fly is most fruitful on freestone streams. It is most likely to be a successful tactic when no major hatch is in progress or during those times when several species are emerging sporadically. You're looking for a situation in which the fish are willing to feed on the surface but are not finely attuned to a particular insect.

Fly selection can be important in this process. Many beginners tend to select flies that are too large. On small streams I'd recommend a #16 dry fly on a 5X tippet as a good size to begin with. A #16 looks small in the fly box but much larger on the water. Even #18s and #20s may be needed as the water falls and clears during the dog days of late summer. On larger streams, a #12 fly on 4X would be a better choice, and a 3X tippet is a good idea on waters where large fish are anticipated. Again, you may need to go to smaller sizes if conditions dictate.

The most popular fly with prospecting anglers is probably the Adams. It's an all-around pattern, good at suggesting a number of possible insects on any water, although it doesn't really "imitate" anything specifically. A fly that I like even better for this fishing is the Dorato Hare's Ear. Designed originally as a caddis imitation, the fly features hackle that is clipped flat even with the hook point so that the fly can be twitched on the surface. The dark coloration of the fly also makes it a good simulator of a number of mayflies and perhaps even of a terrestrial insect.

Speaking of terrestrials, an ant is probably as good a prospecting fly as you can choose for trout fishing. Trout love ants and often choose them when other, even larger insects are on the water. The difficulty with ant patterns is that they are hard to see on the surface, especially in water with some ripple or other surface disturbance. In a glassy pool, however, an ant is hard to beat as a "chuck-and-chance-it" fly.

Whatever the fly you use, it is essential that your leader is stretched and straight before fishing. A leader that is still even slightly kinked or coiled will not unfold properly and cannot be cast with the accuracy that's so critical in pocket prospecting.

ON LIMESTONE CREEKS. On limestone creeks, prospecting with a dry fly is a somewhat more difficult and subtle game than it is on freestone waters. Most of these spring creeks have such a rich food supply that the fish can

Figure 8–3 Three prospecting dry flies. *From the Left*: Ginger Bi-Visible, Adams, Dorato Hare's Ear. Note the natural mayfly in the lower center. (Photo by Katherine G. Lee)

afford to be choosy, and the moderate flow makes it unnecessary for them to hold in heavy current and make quick decisions about a floating fly. Casting into likely areas without actually having located a feeding fish may be counterproductive on such water. A better strategy is to prowl the bank, well back from the water, until you spot a feeding trout or at least a fish holding in such a location that it seems likely to respond to a surface fly. Then make a careful stalk into casting position before making your pitch.

An excellent fly for limestone fishing is a small tie (18-22) of the Blue-Winged Olive pattern. There are several species of mayflies with olive bodies and pale blue-gray wings, and these insects flourish in the silty bottoms and weeds found in limestone streams. On many of these streams, these little flies emerge all summer, especially on drizzly or overcast days, so the fish are quite likely to find such a fly an acceptable offering.

The ant is also an excellent fly for spring creek prospecting, as is the Letort Cricket. The Cricket, in sizes from #12 to #16, is a nice mouthful for a trout. Again, it's a good idea to spot a fish rather than to cast randomly. Sometimes you'll find a relatively large fly like the Cricket refused by limestone trout if they have a long opportunity to scrutinize it. If you get refusals, try dropping the fly just to one side of the fish's head. If the fly lands with a juicy but non-threatening splat, the trout may whirl and take it without giving it a careful once-over.

If you want to fish a Cricket or other prospecting fly but do not see feeding fish, work the edges of weed beds with the fly. On most spring creeks, trout hide back under the edges of the weed mats, and a fly floating along the edge may bring them up with a rush.

You need to use light and long leaders to fish limestone creeks successfully. Sometimes you can get away with 5X when using a large fly like the Cricket, especially if you lengthen the tippet sufficiently. More often you have to go to 6X or even 7X to raise fish in these silken currents. Most experienced spring creek anglers prefer knotless leaders for fishing these waters. The knots on a hand-tied leader collect weeds, and that may cost you a fish. If a good fish takes the leader into the weeds, the debris accumulated on leader knots can soon add up to enough weight to break the leader, regardless of what the fish does. A rod with a moderately soft action is desirable for protecting tippets like these. A stiff rod breaks the fish off when you try to set the hook unless you do so very carefully.

Even more than in the freestone streams, a drag-free float is critical on the limestoners. These waters are generally placid and offer a smoother surface for the trout to look at the fly. They also usually have trailing weeds and other debris that mix the currents and produce many lines of drift of different speeds. Slack line casts are essential, and even then the length of drift without drag is likely to be short. Unlike the

Figure 8–4 A limestone trout about to rise

situation in mountain streams, dragging a fly over a limestone trout is likely to put the fish down for a long period.

Fishing the Rise

Classically speaking, "fishing the rise" is fishing to imitate a hatching insect. In this fishing, you not only locate a feeding fish (or group of them), to which you present your dry fly, but you also try to identify the insect and produce a fly pattern that fools the fish into accepting it as the real insect. It's the classic "matching the hatch" situation.

The first step in this sort of fishing is anticipation. To be successful with any regularity you must be familiar with a given stream and able to predict which flies will emerge at periods when you can be on the stream with an appropriate imitation. Although you will find other fly anglers generous in sharing their information about local hatches, your basic tool in this process is your stream journal, which becomes more valuable as you accumulate new data over the years.

You may also wish to capture and store specimens of insects that populate the streams that you fish. While there are standard fly patterns for matching major hatches, you will find that the coloration of the same insect varies slightly from stream to stream and even from one section of a stream to another. Almost certainly you will begin with a standard pattern, and you will probably catch fish with it. Eventually, however, you may wish to alter the standard recipe slightly to suit location conditions.

As we've seen, there is no shortage of controversy about the best way to imitate an emerging insect. Some authorities emphasize wing outline, some emphasize body color, some demand hackle feathers of the highest quality, others eliminate the hackles altogether. You will undoubtedly find that all these variations in patterns are sometimes effective, but remember that presentation is the most important variable. Even the most artfully tied fly will usually not be accepted by a trout if it does not float naturally. And often an imitation that doesn't look much like the real insect will be taken if it is drifting freely and seemingly unattached.

I had an experience recently that demonstrated this very well. My friend Don Carey and I had journeyed to Chambersburg, Pennsylvania, to fish the Falling Spring Run, a small limestone creek with a well deserved national reputation. We had come to fish to the evening hatch of "sulphurs," which are small, pale yellow mayflies that emerge on this creek in the late spring and early summer. By the time we were able to make the trip, the hatches had been occurring each evening for several weeks. So the fish were well attuned to the natural insect, and the fishing was difficult. Nevertheless, we landed and released two or three fair-sized trout. Then we found the one fish that occupied our time for the remainder of the evening: A fine brown trout, fourteen inches or so long, was rising regularly to the little yellow duns, showing the white lining of its mouth, and making an occasional "smack" as it closed down on one of the helpless insects.

The fish was positioned in the eddy of an outcropping bank, protected from the rear by the trunk of a large tree that had fallen across the creek. The trunk slowed the water, forcing it under the downed portion and creating a pocket with a much slower current than the rest of

Figure 8–5 Two versions of the sulphur (Photo by Katherine G. Lee)

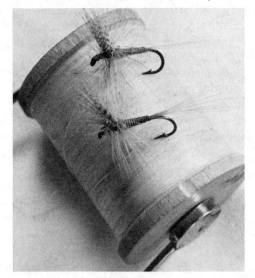

the stream. The fish was holding in this pocket, and, trying as we might, neither Don nor I was able to get an acceptable cast to that fish. No matter how we cast or held our rods, some portion of the leader wound up in the fast part of the creek, and it pulled the fly just enough at the last minute that it floated slightly faster than the natural insects in the same line of drift. Between us, we had five or six variations on the standard sulphur pattern, and a couple of them had already taken fish. The fish rose well twice, only to reject at the last minute when the fly began to pull across the current in an unnatural way. The trout was in a location that made presenting the fly in a natural way impossible, at least for anglers of our level of skill.

We must have worked over that fish for an hour, and we even shared it with two other anglers who strolled by and saw our problem. The most any of us achieved was a curt refusal.

You will probably find, as we did in this case, that as a hatch continues over a period of time the fish feeding to it become more and more "selective" and discriminating with regard to both fly pattern and presentation. This effect usually takes two forms: First, in a single hatch, a fly that takes fish at the beginning may no longer do so as the hatch continues. Second, during an emergence, like that of the sulphurs, that continues for many days, a fly that's effective in May may no longer be reliable in June.

You might attempt to deal with extremely selective fish in several ways. One way is to find fish that are not so selective. You can often find them by moving to a portion of the stream where the surface is roiled enough to disturb the windows of feeding fish, so they cannot make the same precise discriminations as those in the flat water. Another way is to try patterns designed expressly for extremely selective trout. The no-hackle flies developed by Swisher and Richards and the Comparaduns of Caucci and Nastasi are in this category (and in the books recommended at the end of this chapter). Another thing you can try is to switch from the floating dun imitation to a nymph. Often the most selective fish are rejecting your dry flies because they aren't feeding on the duns at all but are taking nymphs floating in the surface film. Look for the bubble in the ring of the rise. If you don't see it, switch to a nymph pattern to represent the hatching insect.

Finally, when all else fails, consider the possibility of a *compound* hatch. Two or more insects are often active at the same time, and the fish sometimes respond to only one species. Often the fly the fish are taking is much smaller than the one you can see on the surface, so you can spend your time meticulously imitating a fly that the fish aren't taking. Use your aquarium net in this situation, and wade right out to where the fish are feeding to get your sample. You can rest the water after collecting your specimen or move on to another stretch. If you manage to hook a fish under these circumstances, the stomach pump will tell you in a hurry what to use. If your vest doesn't contain one of these items, a quick check inside the trout's mouth will often reveal the most recently ingested insects.

On occasion, a fly totally unlike the hatching insect is taken readily, and most anglers can tell a favorite story built around this theme. Unfortunately, prudent anglers just cannot count on this phenomenon. Most of the time you're going to have to match the hatch to some degree.

Although the classic hatch situation is an emergence of floating duns, the spinners can be important too. In many species the spinners fall after it's too dark to see, but fish may still respond to the spinner fly the next morning, when a few dead spinners are still trapped in eddies and slow water pockets.

In a few species, the spinners are more important to the angler than the duns. A case in point is the tiny mayfly belonging to the Caenis family. This insect, the Trichorithodes, is extremely small, imitated by hook sizes 22 to 26. The duns emerge in the morning but molt rapidly, so the spinner fall usually takes place before noon. Hordes of these tiny insects meet over the stream, creating a shimmering cloud in the sunlight as the males and females find each other and mate. Then the females fall to the surface to deposit their eggs, and the feeding of the fish begins in earnest.

The rise of a group of trout to a Trichorithodes spinner fall is an event to be remembered. The fish cruise through the surface with their mouths wide open, taking the swarms of naturals with a gulping action. The angler's fly can easily get lost among the natural insects on the water, and most fishermen try to anticipate the next move that a good trout may make, hoping to place the fly in a location that allows it to be sucked in with a group of the real spinners.

Figure 8–6 Midge drys and nymphs. That's a standard paper match! (Photo by Katherine G. Lee)

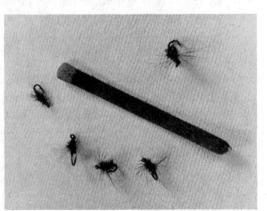

The fishing can be fantastic, and it can also be nerve-wracking in the extreme. Most of the time the fly is invisible, and its location must be guessed. The tiny flies require 6X and 7X tippets; so if the angler gets too anxious, many of the fish are broken off on the strike. On those occasions when the fish can be seen taking the fly and when the barb can be gently drawn back into the jaw of a good trout, the angler is in for a real thrill. I have taken trout up to sixteen inches during this hatch, and many anglers have taken much larger fish with these tiny flies. Such fine and fussy fishing would not be ideal as a steady diet, but it's hard to beat for a peak experience in fly fishing.

Hooking and Holding Fish on Fine Tackle

You'll probably be surprised to discover that relatively large fish can be handled on very light tackle. The main requirements are to relax and to avoid any sudden or hard movements. Light tippets will handle a lot of strain, as long as it isn't sudden or extreme. Tippet material has a capacity to stretch and absorb shock, and longer tippets have more stretch capacity. When you combine a rod with a soft tip and an angler with patience, a heavy fish can be mastered as long as the fish cannot bolt into nearby snags or weeds.

Setting the hook without breaking off the fish is often more of a problem for the beginning angler than playing the fish once hooked. One way to overcome this problem is to use the *slip strike*. As shown in Figure 8–7, the line is circled with the thumb and index finger of the line hand rather than held tightly as usual. Then, when the rod is raised to strike the fish, slack line pays out through the circled fingers with enough resistance to draw the hook into the fish but not enough, hopefully, to snap the tippet.

Figure 8–7 Proper hand-line relationship for the slip strike (Photo by Katherine G. Lee)

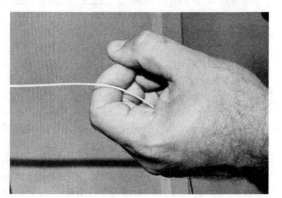

You'll also strike fish more gently if your nerves aren't frayed from trying to find your fly. Many anglers use an indicator on the leader so that they can estimate the fly's location within a small area. A piece of brightly colored fly line, which has been hollowed out and threaded onto the last strand of leader before the tippet, can greatly reduce the area in which you must estimate the fly's location. You might also be able to attach something to the fly that will be visible to you but not to the fish. Some of my friends build a tiny bump of blaze orange wool on the back of the fly, right behind the wing and hackle. With this arrangement, the highly visible material is out of the fish's line of sight but usually visible to the angler.

Finally, tiny hooks work much better if you bend down the barbs before fishing with them. (There are many more good reasons for de-barbing your hooks, as we'll see later.) Bending the hook slightly, so that the point is slightly out of line with the shank, also helps. This slight "offset" widens the effective hook gap, making the point more likely to penetrate.

You've probably heard that an angler should "bow" to a fish that is giving a good tussle. There's more to this rule than good manners. Lowering the rod takes some of the stress off the fine tippet. In fact, it is often essential to point the rod directly at a running fish so that it can take line off the reel without the added drag of the line guides increasing the strain. Many anglers, as you have probably seen, do just the opposite. They raise the rod to the heavens, horsing the fish toward them. This is a fine way to whip a fish when you have heavy tackle, but with the light stuff you must let the fish go where it wants to until it begins to tire. Then, and only then, can you begin to pressure the fish a little. Don't be afraid to use your legs as well as your rod. Follow the fish if necessary and try to get below it if at all possible. A fish that runs upstream will wear itself out rapidly.

Fishing with Terrestrials

Dry fly fishing with imitations of land insects occupies a middle ground between fishing the rise and fishing the water. While terrestrial insects are often present in large numbers (during a flying ant swarm, for example), they are also often taken one at a time by fish feeding opportunistically. And while terrestrial imitations are frequently presented to a feeding fish, they are also excellent prospecting flies.

Terrestrial fishing is a recent development in fly fishing. In the 1940s Vincent Marinaro and his friend Charles K. Fox began experimenting with terrestrial patterns on the Letort and other spring creeks in the Cumberland Valley of Pennsylvania. The two had been frustrated when rising trout refused their carefully tied mayfly patterns, even when offered in tiny sizes. Finally, they discovered that the trout were taking small terrestrial insects, of the family Jassidae, which floated much lower in the surface film than aquatic insects. When Marinaro and Fox began to tie imitations of these creatures, they hooked and landed fish that had previously refused their best efforts. There was a lot more to it, of course, and Marinaro's *A Modern Dry Fly Code* and Fox's *This Wonderful World of Trout* can provide additional details if you're interested.

Unlike mayfly patterns, which are designed to float high in the water, terrestrial flies should float flush in the film of the surface. When hackle is used on these flies it is usually clipped flat on the bottom of the fly so that the body can press into the surface as does the body of the real insect. Indeed, these flies float so low that a rising fish doesn't produce a typical rise form; instead you often see only a bulge in the surface, as if floating nymphs were being taken.

Ants are probably the most essential of the terrestrial patterns on most waters, and sometimes the angler can face a situation in which natural ants are so numerous that the fish become selective to them just as they might to aquatic insects during a hatch. A few years ago I was fishing the Antietam Creek in Pennsylvania one hot afternoon when a sudden storm blew in. My car was close by, so I decided to wait out the lightning and rain. The storm was short but violent, and I returned to the stream to find rising trout everywhere. The Adams that I had been using before the storm was ignored by the fish, and before long I saw why. The surface was littered with ants, washed out of the overhanging trees by the hard rain. I switched to a #14 black ant and landed and released a dozen trout in the next half hour.

While ants, grasshoppers, crickets, beetles, and jassids are the "standard" terrestrial flies, the possibilities are limited only by the

Figure 8–8 A selection of terrestrial dry flies. *From the Left:* Ant, cricket, beetle, grasshopper (Photo by Katherine G. Lee)

imagination of the fly tier. Some anglers fish with housefly imitations, bees, leaf hoppers, inch worms, locusts, and many more. The terrestrial flies have greatly expanded the opportunities to fish with the dry fly.

Bass Bugging

Bass bugs are large surface lures made of plastic, balsa wood, hollow deer hair, or other floating materials. Although bass bugging is not the delicate art that dry fly fishing can be, its specialized tactics are still useful, and they may vary with the species of bass sought.

Bugging for Largemouth Bass

Bass bugging, especially for largemouths, requires tackle somewhat heavier than that used for trout fishing. The bugs are large and air-resistant, and the bass are often found around weed beds, stumps, and other cover where it's easy to get the bug hung up. Heavier equipment allows horsing the fish (or the stuck bug) out of the vegetation and roots.

Bugging for bass is most effective during the spring and fall. In the hot months bugging is most profitable during the early morning and evening hours, when the bass move into the shallows to feed. Many anglers like to fish bass bugs when the fish are on the spawning beds. At that time, a bug that lands nearby will be viciously attacked although protection of the bed is the motive rather than hunger.

Most bass bugs don't imitate anything directly. In fact, many veteran buggers think that the surface disturbance caused by the bug is as much the attraction as the visual qualities of the bug itself. Some bugs have a concave face, so that they push a bubble of water when retrieved. They are called *popping bugs* because of the noise they make when twitched vigorously by the angler. Other bugs are called *sliders* because their rounded heads allow them to glide just under the surface when manipulated.

Largemouth bass often take the bug when it is motionless, so many skilled bass buggers fish their bugs slowly. A widely used technique is to pitch the bug close to cover and allow it to remain still until all the disturbance caused by the landing disappears. Then the bug is twitched just enough to appear to struggle feebly, and then it is allowed to rest again. After the second rest, the bug is retrieved with varying speeds, with pauses, twitches, and pops thrown in. This technique is based on observations of largemouth bass by anglers wearing scuba gear. They have noted that bass often move away warily just after a large object like a popper hits the surface. Then, if it remains still for a moment, they move back toward it to investigate. If the bug then moves again, it may be hit savagely. Like most other techniques, this one doesn't work all the time. Sometimes the bass want more action, other times less. Most anglers start with the technique I've described and experiment from there.

Controlling slack line is a critical aspect of good bugging technique. Most of the manipulations that make the bug pop and gurgle in the water create slack between the rod and the bug. This slack must be kept retrieved so the hook can be set if the bug is taken. You usually have to pull down with your line hand when raising the rod to set the hook. Bass have tough mouths, and the rod alone is not likely to put the hook home, especially if the bug is some distance away when the fish strikes.

Casting a bass bug is different from casting a trout fly. Bugs are heavier than flies, and they offer considerable air resistance to the cast. You'll do better if you slow down your casting stroke and wait a little longer on the backcast than you would ordinarily. With the proper timing a large bass bug can be cast a considerable distance. Most bass buggers who work in weedy waters and who often need to make long casts like rods for 8- or 9-weight lines. And since so much bass bugging is done from boats, a long rod helps to keep the backcast high even when the angler is seated.

Most anglers like bass bug leaders in the six- to eight-foot range. Long leaders are hard to turn over with the air-resistant bugs, and largemouth bass aren't "leader-shy" anyway. Tippets are usually pretty stout; ten-pound test is typical. Although I like a tapered leader for bass bugging, many anglers use a single strand of heavy mono for a leader and get along fine.

If you buy your bugs commercially, be sure that the hook gap is sufficient for setting the hook successfully. Lefty Kreh has developed a good test: Drag the bug across a window screen, and if the hook point doesn't catch in the small holes of the screen, open the gap with pliers until it does.

Bugging for Smallmouth Bass

Smallmouth bass in lakes and impoundments can often be caught on the same bugs and with the same techniques as largemouths. In rivers, however, it can be a different story. The smallmouth is generally more wary and less impulsive than the largemouth, and the loud pops and violent twitches that attract "bigmouths" may only frighten small-mouth. Also, the smallmouth does not require such big bugs as does the largemouth. The smallmouth seems satisfied with smaller mouthfuls that are fished more subtly.

What the smallmouth does like in a bug is action—action supplied by incorporating materials into the bug that move in the water at the tiniest twitch from the angler. I like to tie smallmouth bugs with marabou tails for this reason.

Figure 8–9 Three smallmouth-sized bass bugs (Photo by Katherine G. Lee)

When bug fishing for smallmouths, I like to drop the bug softly and begin a slow, struggling retrieve almost immediately. Although I often throw in pauses, I find that smallmouth bass do not hit a stationary bug as often as largemouth bass do. They like moving food, as long as it's not moving so violently as to be scary. And sometimes, when the fish are in the right mood, you can't move the bug too fast. Again, it's a matter of experimentation. I usually start out with gentle, crippled-looking retrieves and then work up to more violent action if the fish don't respond.

Another very effective technique with both species is to fish your bug with a sink-tip fly line. The sinking tip makes the bug dive when retrieved, but if the bug is buoyant it goes back to the surface during pauses. I like deer-hair bugs with marabou tails for this technique. They look like a sick or injured minnow or a crippled frog, struggling to swim and drifting weakly back to the surface. If you try this just about dusk on a summer evening, hang on to your hat!

Since the smaller bugs are good for smallmouth bass, you can use somewhat lighter equipment than you need for largemouth bass. Most of my friends think I fish too lightly because I like a 6-weight outfit for smallmouth bass bugging. But I want to enjoy the fish I hook to the fullest, so I'll put up with a little more casting difficulty and maybe give up the largest bugs in the process. You'd probably be happier with a 7- or 8-weight outfit.

If you live close to a smallmouth stream, a farm pond, lake, or impoundment, bass bugging may be just the ticket for getting you started in fly fishing. Like fishing with the streamer, bass bugging is hard to do wrong. You are practically certain to catch fish, and a bass on a fly rod can be a real handful.

Whatever the form of surface fly fishing you choose, I hope you feel encouraged to get started in it soon. And while I'm sure that some of the techniques we've discussed in this chapter will be useful, the place to really learn is the water. The fish soon teach you what to do, and you will have that most satisfying of fly fishing experiences: Watching a fish take your fly or bug off the surface. There's nothing quite like it.

Recommended Books

Selective Trout by Doug Swisher and Carl Richards (Crown Publishers, Inc., 1971). Already a modern classic, this book introduced a number of innovative fly patterns, especially the no-hackle dry fly. More than a fly-tying guide, the book is a basic treatise on modern trout fishing with an emphasis on the dry fly. It contains emergence tables for the major mayfly species as well as a key that can be used by the angler to identify specimens captured on the stream.

The Masters on the Dry Fly, edited by J. Michael Migel (J. B. Lippincott Company, 1977). This is an anthology of dry fly fishing, featuring chapters by some of the most skilled anglers in the world. Although slightly uneven in quality, it contains a wealth of information on fishing the dry fly, covering everything from tackle to fly selection to approaching the fish.

The Caddis and the Angler by Larry Solomon and Eric Leiser (Stackpole, 1977). The best of the recent books on fishing the caddis imitations. Although not limited to dry caddis fishing, it contains a lot of information on tying and fishing surface imitations. A good source of fly patterns, too.

Joe Humphreys's Trout Tactics by Joe Humphreys (Stackpole Books, 1981). Joe Humphreys is Professor of Angling at Penn State, following in the footsteps of his mentor, the illustrious George Harvey. Joe calls his book a "meat and potatoes" approach to trout fishing, and that it is. His discussion of dry fly leaders is worth the price of the book, but there is much more, including innovations in weighted flies based on underwater observations. Joe Humphreys is one of the most knowledgable fishermen in the country, and he shares a lot of that knowledge in this book.

9
THE ULTIMATE CHALLENGE:
Fishing the Nymph

I have spent much of this book trying to convince you that fly fishing is easy, readily mastered by the beginner. Yet many people who might well have enjoyed fly fishing have been put off or discouraged due to the mistaken idea that ordinary folks can't master this form of angling. I haven't changed my mind. I still think fly fishing is a basically simple sport in which a beginner can have considerable success right from the start.

If there is an exception to that principle, however, it is fishing the nymph. I might very well say the "art" of fishing the nymph, both for the subtlety of the technique itself and for the respect that I hold for those who have mastered it. Every sport has a pinnacle, an elite level of skill that experts enjoy and novices aspire to. In freshwater fly fishing, nymph fishing is that pinnacle. That doesn't mean that a beginner can't catch fish on nymphs; I not only think you can, I'm going to try to tell you how to do it. But the gap between the expert nymph angler and the beginner is wide, and the gap is closed only by long experience and diligent practice. Developing skill in this most demanding of the fly fishing techniques is the sort of challenge that can become a deep and lasting fascination.

A nymph is a specialized type of wet fly. While the traditional wet flies can be imitative of stream life under certain conditions, this is usually more the result of happenstance than design. Nymphs, on the other hand, are designed to be suggestive of real fish food: immature aquatic insects. A typical nymph has a tail of feather fibers, a fur body, often ribbed with fine wire or a contrasting thread color, and more soft hackle or feather fibers near the head of the fly to represent legs. In many flies a "wing case" is added (usually of a section of flight feather) to add realism to the imitation. Just as important, nymphs are fished in a special way, and successful nymph anglers know the insect they represent with their artificial nymph, and they fish it to mimic the behavior of that insect.

G.E.M. Skues is responsible for nymph fishing as we know it today. A British lawyer, Skues defied the dry fly dogmas of the nineteenth century and demonstrated that fish (in his case, the brown trout of Britain's chalk streams) acquire 85 to 90 percent of their food under the surface. After landing a trout, Skues would open its stomach, pour the contents into a white dish, add water, and stir until the various natural nymphs separated into identifiable specimens. He then tied imitations to match them.

Today Skues' followers still follow practices like this. Modern nymph anglers study stream insects with all the interest of entomologists. They know which insects are active at a particular time of year and in what sections of the stream they are found. They know which nymphs can swim and which can only tumble helplessly in the current if they lose their grip on the bottom rubble. They know the species that spend most of their lives burrowed in the silt and muck of the bottom and that are therefore widely available to the fish only during periods of emergence. They experiment constantly with different shades of fur and synthetic materials, trying to match exactly the color and texture of the natural nymph as it appears in the water. And the more they learn about these and other factors, the more fish they catch.

Nymph Fishing Techniques

A number of techniques of rod handling and fly presentation are useful in nymph fishing, most of which are familiar to you now because they are used in wet fly, streamer, and dry fly fishing. When used with the nymph, these techniques may be slightly modified, but they are generally similar to the practices discussed earlier.

Down and Across

This is the classic presentation of wet fly fishing. The nymph is cast across the stream and allowed to swing below the angler's position, rising and crossing the current as it does so. As with the traditional wet fly, strikes often occur during the "swing" of the fly, but they may occur at other stages of the drift as well.

Up and Across

This is a variation of one of the dry fly techniques. The nymph is cast upstream and to one side of the angler's location, and then it is allowed to drift downstream. Rod manipulation and line retrieve are used to control slack: The rod is raised as the nymph drifts close to the angler's position, stopped at its maximum height as the nymph is directly across current, and is gradually lowered again if the fly is allowed to drift on downstream. Once below the fisherman, the fly swings across the current on the tight line, just as in the down-and-across method. Usually the up-and-across cast is used with a *dead drift*, meaning that the nymph is allowed to drift freely without added motion. In some cases, however, rod twitches and line strips may be added to impart additional action to the fly.

Upstream

In the upstream presentation, the nymph is cast directly upstream and allowed to drift back to the angler's position. The object is to drift the nymph absolutely free. Like the up-and-across technique, the rod is raised and line retrieved as the fly drifts toward the angler. This is generally conceded to be the most difficult of the nymphing techniques because the strike of the fish is very difficult to detect and the nymph is quickly expelled by the fish when discovered not to be real food. Retrieving line and minimizing slack are added complications. Like most difficult techniques this one is deadly effective when carried out by an expert.

Retrieved Nymphs

Many times the nymph is retrieved by the angler, either at the end of a downstream fly swing or as an intentional addition to the fly's action during the drift. A very slow hand-twist or line-weave retrieve can represent the clambering of a live nymph over the bottom. A faster retrieve, even a line strip, can emulate the motions of nymphs that are free swimmers or the emergence or egg-laying of caddis species.

Floating Nymphs

Fishing a floating nymph, rather than a dry fly, during a hatch is often effective. Like the dry fly, the floating nymph is typically fished without added motion.

Drifting nymphs is a technique most common in boat fishing situations. The nymph is simply cast out and allowed to drift freely with the boat. This is an easy way to cover a lot of water with a nymph, and it is also effective in lake situations, where the breeze rather than the current moves the boat around. In river situations the drifted nymph is usually fished without action, but lake fishing with a nymph often calls for a retrieve or other added motion to imitate the behavior common to quiet-water insects.

Nearly all the nymphing techniques are aided by a long fly rod. The long rod allows better line control and also lifts more slack off the surface without requiring an actual retrieve. A long rod also makes it possible to mend line easily, which is even more critical to success with the nymph than in dry fly fishing. A rod with a fairly fast tip action is desirable because it sets the hook more rapidly, a good feature in fishing where the nymph is mouthed cautiously and quickly rejected. Many confirmed nymph anglers like to use graphite rods because of their relatively fast action and because the high stiffness of the material makes it easier to detect a subtle mouthing of the fly. And the light weight of graphite rods also makes it practical to fish a long rod without the penalty of weight and fatigue.

Sinking and Floating the Nymph

In most of the situations you will encounter, the fish will be feeding either at the surface or on or near the bottom. The in-between water offers few feeding opportunities except during a hatch when immature insects are rising to the surface. If fish are not seen bulging on the surface, then you want to sink your nymph deep.

There are several ways to sink a nymph. You can weight the fly in the tying process, or weight the leader with split shot; sometimes you may need to do both. There are advantages and disadvantages to either method. If you weight the fly you sacrifice flexibility; it can never be any lighter again. And some anglers contend that a weighted nymph has a less appealing action than an unweighted one, although I can't verify that from my own experience. On the other hand, if you weight the leader alone the nymph may not sink to the level of the fish, especially in turbulent water. And if you can "feel" anything with this system it will probably be the split shot rather than the fly itself, so you may have difficulty in detecting strikes. The main advantage of weighting the leader is that weight can be added and removed as conditions require.

If you decided to tie or purchase weighted nymphs, you'll need some system for telling the weighted and unweighted ones apart. The differences are so small you won't be able to discern them by feel. Anglers who tie their own flies usually use a different thread color for each type. If you buy your flies you'll probably have to use separate boxes for each.

I add a small amount of weight to most of my nymphs when tying them. Then if additional weight is needed in a particular situation, I can add split shot to the leader.

When you weight the leader rather than the fly, it's a good idea to add the split shot to a dropper strand intentionally tied into the blood knot that joins the tippet to the last strand of the tapered section of the leader. With this method, the shot can be added or removed without disturbing the fly, and you can adjust the depth of the nymph as required by different kinds of water. Another advantage of this system is that the nymph won't hang up on the bottom as much but will drift along slightly off the bottom as the split shots bounce along. And if the shot itself hangs up, you can usually pull it free or break it off without losing your fly. Tie the blood knot so that the dropper material is from the tippet material rather than from the last taper strand. (Note that this is just the opposite of what was recommended in fashioning a dropper for a two-fly cast.) This arrangement makes it easier to break off the dropper when necessary, rather than leaving your tippet and fly in the stream.

In some situations the dropper split shot system is not suitable. If you are fishing on a long tippet, as you will often do in nymphing, placing the shot all the way back at the knot may place it too far away to keep the nymph as deep as needed. In this case you want to add shot directly to the tippet.

Fishing a floating nymph can be a little more complicated. Often it is desirable for the nymph to drift along just under the surface. At other times it will need to float flush in the surface film if it is to represent the buoyancy of the natural insect being represented. Achieving this depth (or the lack of it) may require some experimentation. I like to tie floating nymphs on light-wire dry fly hooks. Then, by using an absorbent fur for the body, I can achieve a near neutral buoyancy in the fly so that it will float right under the surface if the leader is greased with fly floatant. For those nymphs that must float right in the surface, I borrow a trick from my friend Carl Rauer: Carl trims a toothpick to the right size and ties it in under the body of the nymph. Once soaked the fly will float right in the surface film indefinitely, even if you throw rocks at it!

Which Nymphs?

One problem that most beginners face is deciding when to fish with nymphs and which ones to use. Since you usually can't see what's going on under the surface, it's often hard to feel confident that the nymph you've chosen is the right one. I've had conversations with many anglers who were just getting started in nymph fishing, and this is one of the chief complaints. They feel so unsure of which fly to use that they spend more time changing flies than fishing.

If you want to make progress in nymph fishing, you must keep the fly in the water. To do so you need a few flies that you can fish with confidence rather than a wide assortment that only confuses you and promotes indecision. I think most beginners are best advised to choose a few generalized, suggestive nymph patterns and fish them hard rather than trying to use strictly imitative flies and changing them constantly. Here are several patterns that should be successful on almost any trout water:

MAYFLY IMITATIONS. I like three suggestive mayfly patterns: a gray, a medium brown, and a dark brown or black. The gray fly is well represented by the Muskrat nymph. Any fly angler in your area can recommend the best sizes; if you don't know anyone to ask, begin with #10, #12, and #16. The Muskrat nymph suggests scuds as well as some mayfly nymphs, so you can use it on spring creeks as well as freestone streams.

Probably the best all-around nymph is the Gold-Ribbed Hare's Ear. It suggests many of the mayfly nymphs well, and in the larger sizes it can suggest stoneflies and hellgrammites. Get a few in #8 and some in #12, but don't neglect the smaller sizes; a #16 or #18 can be deadly, although few anglers fish them that small. The rabbit ear fur from which the nymph is made is multicolored. When wet, the fly's overall impression is of dark brown, but the Hare's Ear can suggest a lot of shades other than that. This color versatility might be the secret of the fly's success, along with the bristly, scruffy quality that makes the fly look so alive under water.

A good medium brown nymph is the Pheasant Tail. Although not as widely available as the first two, it can be ordered from any local fly tier and is one of the easiest of flies to tie yourself. Made from the fibers

Figure 9–1 Four "impressionistic" nymphs. *Clockwise from the Lower Right:* Gold-Ribbed Hare's Ear, Muskrat, olive nymph, cream nymph. (Photo by Katherine G. Lee)

of ringneck pheasant tail feathers, it is ribbed, like the Hare's Ear, with fine copper wire.

Should you want to go one fly beyond these basics, add a dark olive nymph of some description. The pattern doesn't matter too much as long as olive-brown is the predominant color. This will not only represent many mayflies, but it also can serve as a cress bug in a pinch, especially if you take one of those safety pins and mess it up a little.

One feature that I really like all my mayfly nymphs to have is an overall look of rugged scruffiness. A tightly tied nymph does not have a realistic action in the water, but one with guard hairs, hackle, and other material sticking out becomes "alive" when immersed in water. Most of the commercial nymphs you buy do not have this scruffiness because they don't look good in the display case. Just take a needle or pin and pick out some of the hairs tied down by the tying process, especially along the sides of the nymph where such hairs undulating in the water convey the same action as the gills on a natural nymph. Remember, it's the appearance under water that counts.

CADDIS NYMPHS. Caddisflies are usually represented by the nymph angler in the larval stage. Of the many species of caddis, the majority of them are brown, green, or cream-colored in the larval stage. You can find out which colors predominate on your favorite streams by turning over a few rocks and breaking open the caddis cases you find there. Even if you don't find any bright green ones by this process, carry a couple with you anyway. Many of the free-living (noncase-building) species are bright green, and you might not find them when you turn the rocks over.

Caddis larvae are usually fished dead drift. But when you are imitating the pupae, as you should if an emergence of caddis is in progress, a hand-twist or line-weave retrieve is more effective. Both the Gold-Ribbed Hare's Ear and the Muskrat nymph are good simulators of caddis pupae when fished with added motion.

STONEFLY NYMPHS. Stonefly nymphs are a welcome mouthful for trout (and for smallmouth bass, too) at any time of year. In the West, you'll want a big weighted pattern in black or dark brown (#4 or #6), and for Eastern fishing a small black (#12 or so) and a medium yellow (#8). These flies, fished dead drift, are especially effective in riffle areas where the natural insects are most abundant.

Imitative Patterns

While the generalized patterns I've just described are effective most of the time, on some occasions a carefully tied imitative pattern can be deadly. This is especially productive when a particular species of natural insect is emerging or when it is active just prior to emergence. At these times fish may become finely attuned to the shape, color, size, and behavior of the naturals, requiring an imitation highly similar to the real insect in all these respects.

Particularly critical at such times is a correct match of the color of the real nymph. I believe that color in a nymph is more critical than in a dry fly, simply because the entire fly is submerged under most conditions and readily visible to the fish in all dimensions. Yet many anglers who are fastidious about their dry flies are far less careful with their imitative nymphs. For example, nymph tiers commonly match the colors of the natural nymph with dry fur, even though the color is several shades darker when the fly is wet.

I had my most successful day of trout fishing while fishing an imitative nymph. I had just finished reading a book on fly color called *Fly-Tyer's Color Guide* by Al Caucci and Bob Nastasi. Al and Bob reason that if printers can print full-color photos by mixing tiny dots of only three primary colors, fly tiers ought to be able to mix highly accurate colors by the same process, using fur instead of ink. Their book describes their theory and includes several pages of color charts, as well as their recommended mixtures of red, blue, yellow, and white fur for representing particular insects at various stages in their life cycles. Intrigued, I sent for some of their carefully dyed fur, blended it according to their directions, and tied up several nymphs.

On this particular day I had only a couple of hours to fish, but I expected the nymphs of *Ephemerella subvaria* (commonly known as the Hendrickson) to be active. So I tied three of the *Color Guide* patterns to take along. As I was stringing up my rod along the stream, another angler fished his way through the pool where I planned to begin fishing and then waded across the stream to my side. We shared a few pleasantries

Figure 9–2 A brown trout feeding on emerging nymphs

as he sat down under a tree and took out his lunch. He said that he had caught a couple of trout earlier in the morning but that the past couple of hours had been slow. None too encouraged by his report, I tied on the *Color Guide* Hendrickson and crossed the stream so that I could fish in an upstream direction.

I started to fish in the pool the other angler had just vacated. I cast the nymph into the head of a current line I thought might be productive, saw a flash almost as soon as it entered the water, and hooked a fish. I played and landed the trout, released it, and cast again. Another fish, immediately. The poor fellow sat watching all this, and I was beginning to feel a little embarrassed, especially since my skill (or lack of it) had practically nothing to do with my success. I hooked another fish on my third cast, still another on my fourth and so on, until I had landed seven trout on seven consecutive casts. After the third fish I began to explain to the other angler that this wasn't a typical experience for me, but, as I kept hooking and playing fish all during my explanation, its effect was largely diluted.

Nothing happened on the eighth drift of the nymph through the area, so I moved to the next pool upstream and landed three more trout on three more casts. By this time I was mercifully out of sight of the fellow eating (and probably not digesting) his lunch, so I could settle down and really enjoy this incredible fishing. I caught twenty-three trout before my last *Color Guide* nymph came apart. Then I switched to my regular Hendrickson patterns, fished for a second hour, and caught two more trout.

Thinking this one experience might be a fluke, I returned to the stream several days later when I had just about an hour to fish. I caught seventeen more trout. Two evenings later I accompanied several students from my fly fishing class to the stream. Because I was working with the students, I didn't fish much myself, but I still landed several trout on the fly, and the students, many of whom had never caught trout on a fly before, all caught fish with it.

Whatever that fly had, the fish certainly wanted it, and they were largely indifferent to other patterns intended to represent the same insect. I haven't been able to test the *Color Guide* theory on other species, although I intend to do so soon. Whatever the results of my trials, I will surely never again go near a trout stream at Hendrickson time without a few *Color Guide* nymphs with me.

Strike Detection

Undoubtedly the most frustrating aspect of nymph fishing, for the beginner especially, is the problem of detecting strikes. Actually, the word "strike" is an overstatement; artificial nymphs, especially when they are drifting freely, are usually taken very softly. It can be very disconcerting to have the feeling that your fly is being picked up and expelled by fish without your knowledge.

Skilled nymph anglers usually develop what can only be called a "sixth sense." It's common for experts to answer, "I just know," when asked how they know when to set the hook. They aren't trying to hide secrets; they just can't explain it any further than that. Actually, of course, they are responding to real signals given by the line or leader, but these signals are so subtle that anglers may honestly not know consciously what they are. Nothing but experience can lead you to such expertise that you sense a fish mouthing your nymph without knowing why. Nevertheless, some aids to strike detection can help you pick up many "takes" that might otherwise go undetected.

CONCENTRATION. Although concentration is not a technique or a piece of equipment, it is the basic weapon in the nymph angler's armory. This habit of mind is essential to success with the artificial nymph. Whenever you see a fellow angler on the stream so engrossed in fishing that he or she seems oblivious to everything else, you can bet that fly fisher is using a nymph.

You should focus your most careful attention on the point where the line or the leader goes under the surface. If there is to be any visible indication of a fish's take, you will see it there. The line or leader pauses, moves upstream slightly, or moves downstream faster than the current. If any such thing happens, set the hook. Often you will hook only the bottom, but this should not discourage you. It proves that you did detect some interruption in the drift of your nymph, and it also shows that your nymph is working in the right area. If you don't hang up the nymph or your split shot occasionally, your nymph is probably not down where the fish are.

While concentrating on the point where the line goes under, be alert for any indications of fish moving under the surface. Usually a fish turns slightly when taking a nymph, and this movement may be betrayed by a subtle flash of white belly. This "wink under water," as Skues called it, should always be met by a strike by the angler, whether or not you think the nymph is in that area. Don't take your eyes off the line point you're concentrating on so that you can see this indication of a take; I've found that the flash will be detected just as readily, perhaps more so, when you're not looking for it or directly at the point where it occurs. All you need to do is keep in mind that this wink often happens; if it does, you'll see it.

STRIKE INDICATORS. You might find it easier to focus your attention if you make use of a strike indicator. One of the major fly line companies makes a floating line called the Nymph-tip, which has a fluorescent orange bulb at the very end of the line. The bulb makes it very easy to follow the point of the line–leader junction even at a distance. Although I personally don't find such a line necessary for small stream nymphing, I do use the Nymph-tip in river nymphing for smallmouth bass. It's a great help when the line tip is a long way from the angler.

Another item offered by the same company, called the Striker, is a small fluorescent foam patch that can be folded around the leader. The Striker offers a highly visible reference point that can be readily moved to any part of the leader.

You can also make a home-made strike indicator, like the one recommended for following tiny dry flies on the surface. Take a small section of fly line that is bright in color, hollow it out by pushing a needle through the core (heating the needle slightly helps), and thread it on the section of leader that you want to concentrate on. If you use knotless leaders, you might need to tie a knot just under the indicator to keep it from sliding down too far. If you tie your own leaders, you can build strike indicators into them initially or add them on the stream to suit conditions. The disadvantage of this home-made indicator is that it can't be moved easily from one section of the leader to another. But the price is right!

A final method of strike detection is using a dry fly as an indicator. Add a dropper at the appropriate point on the leader, tie on a high-floating dry fly, and use it as a bobber just as you would with a bait fishing outfit. Not only will the bobber/fly aid in your detection of pickups of your nymph, but your concentration on it will help you learn to read currents and lines of drift more skillfully. And since you will occasionally take a fish on the dry fly you have the benefit of added fishing excitement. The only disadvantage of this method is that the dry fly must be at the proper point on the leader to work well as a bobber. If it's too far up the leader, the dropper stand will develop so much slack that the dry fly may not show the pause or twitch when the nymph is taken. If it is too close to the nymph, it may interfere with the natural drift of the nymph on the bottom. The dry fly bobber is best suited to streams of moderate and relatively uniform depth, when you can locate the bobber properly once and leave it there.

Whatever the method you choose, your concentration will be aided if you compare your reference point with other material floating on the surface. Bits of foam, leaf matter, or other debris will serve; compare the speed and direction of your reference point with that of the flotsam floating around it. When you see deviation, strike!

One day you will find yourself raising the rod without knowing why and feeling the weight of a fish on the other end. That is the ultimate experience of the nympher. When it happens to you, you'll know you're on the way to becoming a skilled nymph fisherman. And I'll bet you'll be a nympher for life.

Let's try to integrate some of the information we've discussed thus far
and apply it to real fishing situations.

"Prospecting" with the Nymph

You prospect with the nymph when you don't see fish feeding on
the surface and when no important hatch is in progress. You may see fish
taking nymphs down deep or spot their tails breaking the surface as they
do so, but you do not know exactly what nymphs they are feeding on. In
most situations where the prospecting nymph is used, you don't see fish
at all.

Under these circumstances you want to turn to the suggestive
nymphs. To choose the one to start with, turn over a few stones or dig up
the bottom a bit (being careful not to disturb too much of the streambed)
and examine the nymphs that you find. Dark wing pads indicate that the
nymphs are mature and that a hatch is not too far away, so attempt to
generally match any nymphs that you find with this feature. They will be
active and the fish will respond to them. If you don't spot any indications
of a coming emergence, then pick a fly that matches the general color
and size of the most common nymph that you collect.

Unless you know that the nymphs you have examined are of the
free-swimming varieties, you will probably do best to begin by fishing
your artificial without added motion. I usually prospect with the up-
and-across method because it combines many of the best elements of the
other techniques. Weighting the leader if necessary, cast the fly well
upstream of your target so that it can sink deeply before it reaches the
suspected lie of the fish. Drift it abreast of your position and on downstream, raising the rod and retrieving line as necessary to keep slack to a
minimum. Mending line at intervals is often necessary to secure a long,
drag-free drift. As the fly tightens on the downstream line, raise the rod
tip and wiggle it from side to side a few times. You may hook a fish when
you raise the rod at this point, so I have developed the habit of making a
slight hook-setting lift at this point, even if I haven't really detected a
take. Since this lift and the accompanying wiggle represent the action of
an emerging nymph headed for the surface to hatch, this action adds
appeal to the fly even if no fish is mouthing it at the time.

After the drift is completed it is sometimes effective to retrieve the
fly with a slow hand-twist or line-weave. Experimentation is the key to
effective prospecting with the nymph.

You will find this general tactic effective under many conditions.
153   In the early spring a weighted stonefly is very effective with this presen-

tation. Later in the season small mayfly nymphs are successful. In spring creeks an olive or Muskrat nymph fished in this way will take fish, and, if you have a cress bug or scud imitation, so much the better. If you see caddisflies in the air, you might try the Hare's Ear, with extra time devoted to the tight-line portion of the drift and a line-weave retrieve thrown in. You can catch a lot of small- to medium-sized smallmouth bass using this method, especially with a Hare's Ear or caddis larva pattern in #8 or #10. You might even catch a big smallmouth if you tie a hellgrammite imitation to your leader. In short, prospecting with the nymph will be your most frequent tactic, and the up-and-across presentation is usually the most useful approach.

Fishing the Nymph During a Hatch

The period prior to and during an emergence can be the most productive time to fish a nymph. Most anglers turn to the dry fly at this time. But many fish continue to feed on the nymphs throughout the hatch and are not likely to take a dry fly, no matter how well presented and imitative. Then, too, on many hard-fished streams the larger fish become quite selective and cautious after seeing so many dry flies drifted over them. Yet these fish may be ready candidates for a nymph fished during a hatch.

Generally speaking, you need to fish an imitative nymph during a hatch. Its size, of course, is basic, but as I indicated earlier I have come to believe that color is just as critical during these times. Capturing a specimen of the insect is essential to accurate representation.

If you find yourself without an appropriate nymph, see what you can do to alter the ones you have to make them more closely approximate the natural. You might be able to trim a large fly down to size with your scissors, and if you pick out the body of a little nymph it will look a lot bigger in the water. You might think that color alterations are beyond your capabilities while on the stream, but that's not entirely true. You can always darken your flies if you carry a couple of waterproof marking pens in your vest, and sometimes that can make all the difference in the world. I carry light brown, medium brown, and black markers, and I find that they help in many situations. A cream nymph can be turned into a light brown with the light brown pen or darker brown with the medium brown pen. The shade of an olive nymph can be altered appreciably with the light brown marker. The black pen can be used to darken the thorax area of your flies if you find the naturals with the dark wing pads mentioned earlier and don't have the flies to match them. Remember that it's the color when wet that matters, and be sure to get the waterproof pens. The regular ones will wash off in a cast or two.

If you expect a hatch that has not yet begun, it's a good bet to fish an appropriate nymph deep. Once the hatch has begun, however, you'll probably need to switch to the floating nymph fished in or just under the surface film.

Floating nymphs should be tied on dry fly hooks and the leader greased so that most of it floats. If you have already fished deep with a given leader, change to a dry one and then grease it with fly floatant to within a foot or so of the fly. You can experiment from there to determine if additional greasing is needed to make the fly ride even higher.

The floating nymph fished during a hatch is almost always presented upstream as if it were a dry fly. The dead-drift float is also typical, although at times a slight twitch of a floating nymph can be deadly. Usually the take of the fish can be seen, although often you cannot tell whether your nymph or a natural one has been ingested. As usual, if in doubt, strike. Watch the floating portion of the leader to help you make sure which rises are to your fly.

As in other nymphing situations, a long and supple tippet can make a lot of difference, and careful casting is also essential. Usually, it is necessary to present the fly without having shown the leader to the fish, especially in slow water, so working on the curve cast benefits you.

Once you have successfully fished a nymph during a hatch, you may not want to go back to the dry fly. With the right nymph and a good presentation, the floating nymph is one of the most effective of all fly fishing tactics.

Fishing the Midge Nymph

Sometimes on trout streams you see fish rising and feeding heavily, but you cannot see any hatch in progress or any mayflies or caddisflies in the air. You may also note that many of the trout are not rising in typical fashion but coming up out of the water like porpoises, showing their backs rather than their heads. If so, you are probably observing a midge hatch. Fishing a dry fly during such emergences is sometimes effective (a dry midge pattern is included in the Appendix), but more often the fish respond best to imitations of the emerging pupae.

To interest fish under these conditions you need tiny nymphs fished on extra-long and light leaders. These little nymphs are simple to tie because the pupae themselves are not large or very complicated. Usually a tiny fur body with a turn of something fuzzy at the head does nicely. Midge pupae come in a variety of colors, so you need to inquire of other anglers or catch some of the little critters yourself to match the hatch. If you choose the latter route, don't bother with your nymph net—you need a handkerchief!

The standard floating nymph technique is used during a midge hatch. Grease the leader down close to the fly, and cast so the nymph comes over the fish before the leader. You will usually see the fish take, but be careful that you don't strike too soon. The fish usually takes the nymph on the way down, so if you strike when you see the fish rise you may pull the fly away before it is taken. You must strike delicately due to the tiny size of the fly and the light leader tippets (usually 7X). As with the tiny dry flies, bending the hook shank slightly to an offset from the point helps to insure more hookups.

An emergence of these Diptera presents the nymph angler with one of the most challenging of fly fishing situations. It calls for highly refined tackle and technique, but the rewards can be exciting.

Summing Up

If your first few attempts at fishing the nymph are not as successful as you would like, don't get discouraged. I delayed my own progress for years by switching quickly to other types of flies whenever my nymphs did not produce immediately. I finally taught myself to fish nymphs (after a fashion) by leaving my other flies at home. Then, and only then, did I fish my nymphs with the persistence that was required for success. You will probably have more will power than I did, but if you find yourself switching to a fly that you have more confidence in, this self-imposed form of discipline might work for you too.

Whatever system eventually leads you to success with the nymph, it will be an accomplishment that gives you real satisfaction. While skilled nymph fishing by itself will not qualify you for the title of "expert," you certainly cannot claim that dubious title without developing skill in this form of fly fishing. Ultimately your own satisfaction is the measure by which you gauge your fishing, and catching fish on nymphs can be satisfying indeed. Seeing a fish turn for your nymph as it drifts along and setting the hook into a deceived trout are true joys of fly fishing.

Recommended Books

Nymphs by Ernest Schwiebert (Winchester Press, 1973). Considered by many to be the most complete book available on nymphs and nymph fishing. It covers mayflies, caddisflies, stoneflies, and midges, and it features Schwiebert's color illustrations of the nymphs as well as elaborate fly patterns. Although the book sometimes tells you more than you want to know, it is a basic book for the nymph angler.

Nymph Fishing for Larger Trout by Charles Brooks (Crown Publishers, Inc., 1976). Explicit, no-nonsense instruction on nymph fishing. Particularly useful for the Western angler, Brook's straightforward book is one of the best available on nymph fishing techniques.

10
THE BARBLESS HOOK

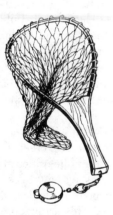

One morning a few years ago I joined several of my fishing friends on a stream on the outskirts of the town where I work. It was the opening day of trout season, but we were not there to fish. Our fly fishing club had been asked to cooperate with the state department of natural resources in gathering information about the other anglers fishing that morning. Our job was to distribute questionnaires to the fishermen as they left the stream, to assist them in filling them out, and to collect the questionnaires before they left for home.

We arrived before daybreak and found the highway lined with cars and the stream lined with anglers. The creek had been stocked with hatchery trout a few days before, and the fishermen were anxious for the opening hour to arrive so they could legally begin fishing.

Six o'clock arrived, and the various baits hit the water. Worms, cheese, corn, salmon eggs, and more were used, and all were successful. By 6:01 A.M. half the rods in view had bends in them, and by 6:15 the first anglers were beginning to leave, having caught their limit of trout. They hurriedly filled out the forms we thrust on them and went on their way. Many said they never fished for trout except for those few minutes at the beginning of the season. One fellow who didn't leave until about seven said he didn't intend to come again if it was going to take a whole hour "to catch five lousy trout." By eight most of the cars were gone and only a few fishermen were left on the stream, most of them kids who moved into productive spots after the older anglers had left. Our job done, my friends and I headed for home considerably earlier than we had expected.

Later that same day I had to pick up some supplies at a shopping mall near my home. While making my way toward the hardware department of a department store, I noticed a large crowd in another section of the store. So I ventured over to see what all the excitement was about. The store was holding what was billed as a "fishing rodeo" (though why fishing ought to be described as a "rodeo" I have no idea) to promote the sale of fishing gear. A plastic swimming pool had been installed in place of two merchandise shelves, and in the pool were several dozen small trout. For fifty cents passersby could rent rods and reels, bait up with the worms provided, and catch themselves some trout. And they would catch a trout; the fish had been carefully starved so they would take the bait even under such absurd conditions. I spoke to a salesman who was leaning on a long-handled net. When I asked the purpose of the net, he explained that it was insurance against "any of these kids going away disappointed."

I stayed and watched for a while. I had seen these promotions before, but I had never taken the time to really consider what was going on. The longer I thought about it, the more incredible it seemed. Suppose, I asked myself, the store had decided to promote the sale of hunting equipment by arranging for customers to rent .22-caliber rifles and shoot live rabbits held in a cage? Would there not have been a public outcry? And would not sportsmen have been in the forefront of those protesting such brutal and unsportsmanlike marketing tactics? And yet there was no outcry here at the "rodeo." Everyone acted as if catching starved trout in a plastic swimming pool in the middle of a shopping mall was the most natural thing in the world, or at least a fun way to spend part of a Saturday afternoon.

Gradually it occurred to me that what I was witnessing here was simply a smaller-scale version of what I had seen on the creek that morning. Perhaps that is why there has never been public criticism of what the store was doing that day. For a host of reasons, we have become used to the idea that tame and stupid fish should be made available to the public on a regular basis, announced in advance. This arrangement many people regard as a proper way of satisfying the urge for sport.

If you're like most fly fishermen, you've already passed through the "opening day" stage. Perhaps you're planning to skip it altogether. You enjoy catching fish, of course, but you want to do it under challenging conditions where the fish can be at their best. Trout fresh from the hatchery that race to the bank in anticipation of a handout when the first angler appears don't qualify.

This is not to say that stocking programs and "put-and-take" fishing are to be condemned. Some persons enjoy this sort of fishing, and they are as entitled to their preferences as we are to ours. It's also a fact that many of the streams stocked with hatchery trout cannot support fish long enough for anything besides put-and-take fishing to be practical. Fly rodders, however, want to fish for trout in a stream that can support the fish for long periods, a stream with natural insect life to imitate, ideally a stream that can allow some natural reproduction. They would prefer to fish for "wild" trout if possible, but if not they want the hatchery fish to have a period of time to become "stream-wise" before they become their quarry. And they want some trout to be there all season.

In short, fly anglers want a "quality" fishing experience, and while we may disagree on what that is, there is no disagreement on what it is not: It is not put-and-take fishing, whether that takes place in a creek or in a plastic swimming pool in a department store.

Catch-and-Release

One way to improve the quality of fishing in many waters is for the anglers who fish there to release many of the fish that they catch. *Catch-and-release* fishing has become popular in many areas, and the reason is clear: More quality fishing becomes available for more anglers when some or most of the fish caught are released to strike and fight again.

For the present, the catch-and-release streams around the country are trout streams, for a number of reasons. Trout are very popular with anglers of all persuasions, and most trout streams cannot support the pressure of many fishermen, all expecting to catch and to keep a limit of trout each day they fish. Perhaps equally important is the fact that in most states where there are trout streams the state raises fish in hatcheries and deposits them in streams. Since the state raises the fish, the state can readily establish regulations governing how they are used, subject, of course, to political pressure from sportsmen's groups and individuals.

While there are not yet any catch-and-release rules for species other than trout, the method is practiced with other species. Many largemouth bass anglers voluntarily practice catch-and-release, and some of the tournaments that bass fishermen compete in require fish to be kept in live wells and then released once the tournament is over. In Virginia two of the state's best smallmouth bass rivers have operated under special regulations for several years because of mercury contamination. The Governor has ordered that fish from these rivers cannot be kept for human consumption. Since sport fishing continues, the effect of contamination has been the creation of a catch-and-release fishery for smallmouth bass. The fish are thriving, and most anglers agree that the fishing has never been better from a sporting standpoint. These developments, happenstance though they may be, suggest that catch-and-release angling can be extended to species other than trout with equally good results.

Generally, some "special regulations" are combined with the catch-and-release approach. Angling is usually limited to fly fishing and/or spinning. In some locations barbless hooks are required. Although the specifics vary, the goal is to assure that fish are caught by some method known to be relatively harmless, so that those released will recover to provide sport in the future.

Quite often special regulations include the opportunity to keep certain fish. Most typical are "trophy fishing" regulations, which allow the retention of a fish or two per day over a certain size. In other locations, a fish or so *below* a certain size can be kept, to assure that trophy fish remain in the stream to pass along their fast-growing traits to subsequent generations.

Since catch-and-release fishing is still fairly new, it is not yet certain which regulations work best in protecting and improving the fishing. Much of the present work is still in the experimental stages and is subject to revision by aquatic biologists who collect and analyze data to assess the impact of certain restrictions. Each stream is different, and so it requires a unique approach. The most progressive states have special regulations designed for particular streams rather than state-wide rules.

Catch-and-release fishing is controversial. Many bait fishermen see it as an elitist practice, designed to favor the fly fishermen, and they often fight the attempt to impose special regulations on a stream that has a history of unrestricted trout fishing. The regulations, however, are not designed to favor one group over another. The simple fact is that trout caught on bait and hardware do not survive after release in sufficient numbers to justify allowing the use of these techniques in catch-and-release areas. Fish caught on flies, on the other hand, nearly always survive if handled properly. If fly fishing did not already exist, it would have to be invented before catch-and-release fishing could become feasible.

Yet the objections of bait fishermen have made it difficult to convert many otherwise promising streams to catch-and-release. One result is that in most states the "flies only" or catch-and-release areas represent a very small portion of the total trout water, and many of these streams are overcrowded with fly anglers looking for a quality angling experience and having no place else to go.

Needless to say, most fly fishermen hope for more catch-and-release trout water, and many angling clubs and conservation organizations are working toward this goal. Most anglers recognize, however, that they cannot succeed by depriving other fishermen of their sport. And many streams cannot support special regulations. The solution is education, both of the general public and often of the leadership of the natural resources departments, some of whom are political appointees with little special knowledge of fishing or aquatic biology. Bait anglers also have the option of learning to fly fish themselves, and more of them are doing so all the time. They are usually taught to fly fish by anglers already committed to the catch-and-release philosophy.

Perhaps you haven't yet made up your own mind about catch-and-release fishing. Fish are good to eat, and they are fun to show off. And there is something in most of us that wants tangible proof of our skill. But one thing is certain: Unless you live in the backwoods of Maine or in the wilds of Alaska, if you want quality fly fishing for trout, you'll have to accept and support catch-and-release regulations. In most of the country, there's no other way to make the sport available to everyone.

Releasing Fish

Releasing a fish might seem so simple that no explanations ought to be necessary. It's true that letting a fish go is no great skill, but letting one go with a good chance of survival is another matter. Too many fishermen literally "throw them back" and consider themselves catch-and-release anglers. There's more to it than that.

Successful catch-and-release fishing begins before the fish is landed. The first rule of the catch-and-release angler is to play the fish efficiently so that it can be landed and released before it becomes completely exhausted. Studies show that when fish are played for long periods they accumulate high levels of lactic acid in their tissues. This accumulation can reach fatal levels, especially in water that is unusually hot or lacking in oxygen. An overplayed fish may appear well enough upon release only to die later on from the exhausting experience.

Playing the fish efficiently means that the fishermen must develop skill in using light tippets and sometimes must forego use of the lightest leaders if their use would prolong the playing time to a dangerous degree.

One of the reasons that fly fishing is so well suited to catch-and-release is that flies are seldom taken deeply and are usually easy to remove without undue stress to the fish. Yet there are exceptions, most often with streamers and bucktails. If a fly is deeply imbedded and difficult to reach, cut the leader and release the fish with the fly still imbedded. The acid in the fish's system will eat away the hook point and barb, and the fly will be expelled in a few days. At least the odds for survival are better than they would be if you manipulated and wiggled the fly in an effort to get it free. Such manipulation often causes bleeding, and studies show that bleeding fish seldom survive after being released. Some other studies show that when bleeding fish (largemouth bass in this case) return to a school, the other fish immediately cease feeding and become very wary. So if you land a bleeding fish, and the regulations allow it, keep that one for the pan.

You will find releasing fish much easier if you use barbless hooks. These hooks are available commercially, but it is difficult to find them in all the sizes and types that fly fishermen use, so most anglers bend down the barbs on their hooks with pliers. When done properly, this leaves a little bump where the barb was.

Contrary to what many fishermen believe, the barb doesn't add much to the holding power of most hooks. I have been fishing with barbless hooks almost exclusively for years and have not noticed any increase in unhooking since I went the barbless route. If anything, angling success increases because with no barb the point of the hook penetrates better, resulting in fewer missed strikes.

Finally, one of the most important virtues of a barbless hook is that it can be removed from the *angler* quickly and safely. More than one fishing trip has been rerouted to the emergency room when a barb got in past the skin surface. It is practically certain that you'll hook yourself (or someone else) at some point in your angling career. I hope it will be with a barbless hook.

When using barbless hooks, releasing your fish without touching it or lifting it from the water is usually possible. You simply reach down and grasp the fly, and with a twisting motion, pull it free. With a barbed hook, on the other hand, the fish must be handled, and removing the fly is often maddeningly difficult. This is especially true with tiny hooks. They offer so little overall mass that it's difficult to get enough leverage to pull them out. This is another reason to use barbless hooks: With the barbed ones you often have to cut the leader and let the fish go with your fly rather than subjecting it to undue stress. With barbless hooks, you'll get to use your little flies more than once!

The use of barbless hooks is not limited to trout fishing or even to catch-and-release fishing. If you hook more fish with barbless hooks, you will land more fish with barbless hooks. I've been using barbless hooks (except for streamers) on smallmouth bass for a couple of years, and while a leaping smallmouth will sometimes spit the fly back at me, they were doing that anyway long before I turned to barbless hooks. You might try bending the barbs on your sunfish hooks too; many of this group like to eat morsels almost exactly the size of their mouths, and if that morsel happens to be your popping bug you'll have a hard time getting it loose. With a barbless hook, all you need to do is to push the bug in a little farther and then pull it straight out.

You often hear it said that a barbless hook comes out the instant a fish is given some slack line. I haven't found this to be generally true. In fact, I used to try to release the little ones that way; I'd give slack and wait for them to swim off the hook. A few of them did, but in most cases I waited so long for them to free themselves that I decided it was less stressful to land them and then let them go. You'll find that most of the time a fish that is hooked well stays hooked, barb or no.

Sometimes, even with barbless hooks, you have to handle the fish to remove the fly or to revive the fish after a long tussle. Although there remains some controversy about it, most authorities agree that it is best to handle fish with wet hands so that the protective mucous that covers their scales will be less disturbed. The problem is that the combination of slippery fish and wet hands makes it very likely that the fish will be dropped and injured, especially since the handling is usually a one-hand operation.

Trout are particularly slippery, and their streamlined shape makes them hard to get a grip on. I find a trout easier to handle if I lay the rod down and do not try to lift the fish from the water. While holding the trout on either side of the head, you can usually remove the hook. While you should avoid squeezing the fish even here, the bony structure of the head and skull can stand more pressure than the midsection. Many trout are fatally injured by being held too tightly around the middle. Be careful not to get your fingers into the gills; gill injuries are usually fatal to the fish.

Bass are handled most easily while being held by the lower lip. Insert your thumb into the fish's mouth and grasp the bottom lip with your thumb inside and your index finger outside. As you lift the fish, you immobilize it with no ill effects. The lip hold is very secure and has the advantage of disturbing very little of the protective slime on the bass.

Members of the panfish family usually have mouths too small for the lip hold, but be alert for a large specimen that could be handled this way. Otherwise panfish are usually held with the fingers over the back and the thumb under the belly. Be careful to start your fingers at the front of the dorsal fin and fold it down as you slide your hand back; otherwise you'll get a painful sting from the sharp tines of that fin.

Some anglers find it easier to release fish using a landing net. They say the net makes it possible to hold the fish firmly without ever letting it out of the net—you just grasp the net, fish and all. Once the fly is removed, the net is immersed again and the net bag reversed. The fish then swims away.

It sounds really easy, and I hope if you try it that it works out that way for you. When I do it I can't find the fly for the net. And, when I get the fly free of the fish, it immediately fouls in the net, and the fish gets so tangled in the process that it can't get free when I put the net back in the water. Of course, I'm clumsier than average. The other problem with the net is that the cords of the net bag strip the protective mucous off the fish, especially when the bag is used to grasp the fish. So, while I sometimes carry a net in the hopes of hooking a trophy (it hasn't happened yet), I land and release my fish by hand. Even if you decide to use a landing net regularly, you should practice landing and releasing fish by hand.

Reviving an Exhausted Fish

Sometimes even prudent playing and landing result in a badly exhausted fish. One of the best indications of true exhaustion is the fish's turning over in the water, or "going belly up" in angler jargon. Such a fish needs artificial respiration if it is to survive.

To revive such a fish, first remove the hook. If the fly is deeply imbedded and if it appears that removing the hook requires prolonged manipulation, cut the leader and leave the fly. In a severely exhausted fish, a small hook is less dangerous than additional stress. Your first priority is to get the fish free and to get to work reviving it.

The next step in the resuscitation process is to create a flow of water over the fish's gills. This raises the oxygen level in the blood and reduces the level of lactic acid. If you are in a current area, all you have to do is hold the fish gently with the head in an upstream direction. If you are in quiet water, you need to move the fish back and forth, forcing water over the gills. Holding the fish quietly in current is much better, so move to a current area if at all possible.

There is no need to hold the fish tightly; it will be too exhausted to escape. One hand supporting the belly and another softly over the back is sufficient to hold the fish in place. You will feel strength return to the fish, but continue to hold it gently. If a feeble struggle frees the fish from your grasp, gently capture it again and continue the process. When the fish is recovered, it will be able to swim strongly from your grasp. In fact, you won't be able to hold it even if you try. Let the fish release itself, and don't stop the reviving process until it can do so. This whole process may take several minutes, especially if it has been necessary to play the fish for a lengthy period or if stream conditions are poor. I have worked for five minutes or so on several fish, and it's worth the effort. When the fish breaks from your grasp and swims strongly away, you feel one of the real gratifications of the catch-and-release angler.

Organizations for Fly Fishermen

If you remain interested in fly fishing, you will probably join one of the clubs that have sprung up all over the country. While some of these clubs are local and independent, many are affiliated with one or both of the two major national organizations to which many fly anglers belong:

Trout Unlimited and The Federation of Fly Fishers (formerly the Federation of Fly Fishermen).

Trout Unlimited

Trout Unlimited (or TU) was founded in Michigan in 1959. Modeled on the already established Ducks Unlimited, TU was founded by anglers interested in preserving and restoring trout habitats and advancing trout fishing as a sport. TU has grown into a major national organization, with regional councils coordinating hundreds of affiliated clubs. And while the organization has not affirmed fly fishing as the best method for catch-and-release fishing (in spite of all the evidence that it is the best method from a mortality standpoint), the emphasis is clearly on management of the trout resource with conservation as a primary concern.

True, many fly fishermen are disappointed that TU has not made the commitment to fly fishing that seems justified by what has been learned about trout and trout fishing methods since 1959. It is equally true that many anglers in leadership positions in TU chapters all over the country are enthusiastic fly fishermen, committed to fly angling as the best and most sporting method of trout fishing. Whatever the doctrinal disputes, Trout Unlimited clearly works for the trout and for the preservation of quality trout fishing. Those are objectives that fly fishermen can support.

The Federation of Fly Fishers

The Federation of Fly Fishers (FFF) was founded in Eugene, Oregon in 1965. The majority of affiliated clubs are still found on the West Coast, although strong development in the Rockies, Midwest, and East has taken place in the last few years.

The Federation is strictly a fly fishing organization, and it strongly stresses the fly rod as the proper tool for trout and salmon fishing. FFF has also been a leading influence not only in the development of saltwater fly rodding, but also in encouraging the use of the long rod in other angling areas.

Although the two groups continue to disagree about the role of fly fishing in trout management practices, FFF and TU have cooperated more and more on the national level in recent years. Many fly fishing clubs around the country are affiliated with both groups. Invariably, two organizations with such similar goals and philosophies will cooperate still more in the future, and many anglers devoted to both groups hope for an outright merger.

Incidentally, you can join each of these organizations on an individual basis for a small yearly membership fee. With payment of the fee comes a patch, a decal or two, regular newsletters, and subscriptions to the quarterly magazines published by each group. You may also support TU and FFF by joining affiliated clubs.

The Brotherhood of the Jungle Cock

This is not a major national organization, but it is one that I am personally involved in and that I hope to see prosper. The Brotherhood, founded in 1940 by three Maryland anglers, takes its name from the colorful Indian fowl that was once a staple of fly-tying materials. (Jungle cock plumage cannot be imported any longer and is today quite rare.) The Brotherhood has the distinction of being the first conservation organization to incorporate a catch-and-release philosophy. Members take a pledge, in the form of the Jungle Cock Creed, in which they agree always to limit their catches to *less* than the legal limit.

The most important function of the Brotherhood, and its reason for being, is the transmission of the love of fishing to the coming generations. Each year a "Campfire" weekend is held, and each member who attends must bring a youngster. Under the guidance of their sponsors, they are taught angling skills by experienced fishermen and simultaneously taught to love and respect the environment. Apart from those duties, voluntarily taken on by the leaders of the organization, there is but one obligation of membership: for at least one weekend a year "to take a boy a-fishing."

While the Brotherhood is not an exclusively fly fishing organization, fly fishing skills are given heavy emphasis in the instructional program, and the training of the young in concern for the environment is a task that fly fishermen have always assigned a high priority.

In Conclusion . . .

If you have come with me this far, I hope that you now feel confident that you can go out and catch fish with fly equipment. Perhaps you've already found that you can succeed with these techniques. If not, I hope that you will soon. I also hope that, as you become experienced in fly fishing, you come to know some of the associated pleasures that fly anglers enjoy: the friendships, the conservation work, the organizations, the fine books, the memories collected over the years.

I suspect that you have come to fly fishing because you already know that fishing means more than fish. I hope your understanding of that grows with the years, as mine has done. I hope too that you will keep a sense of perspective about your fishing. Fly fishing is fascinating, and I have known an angler or two who lost the sense of perspective that in the end keeps the game the pleasure that it is. The line between interest and obsession is a thin one, and many of us who fish with flies have crossed it at one time or another. I hope that you will belong to the majority who cross it seldom and come back always.

Ultimately, fly fishing is neither a discipline, nor a calling, nor a philosophy, but a way of having fun. So I wish for you a long life of fishing—just difficult enough to make your successes all the more gratifying.

Have fun.

APPENDIXES

A
BASIC
FLY PATTERNS

This appendix includes a list of thirty-five basic fly patterns and their dressing instructions. These flies are reliable (in many cases, classic) patterns that catch fish in all areas of the country.

The following basic information will help you to interpret the pattern recipes accurately:

HOOKS. Hook size is based on the distance between point and shank—the *gap*. Dry flies are usually tied on light-wire dry fly hooks, and wets on heavier hooks. An "X" in the hook designation means "extra," and it is interpreted based on the information that precedes and follows the X. So a "2X long" hook has a shank as long as a standard hook two sizes larger; for example, a "2X long" #14 would have a shank as long as a standard #10. A 2X stout would be a heavy hook, made of a wire diameter typically used in a hook two sizes larger. The numbers given in parentheses are the model numbers for Mustad hooks.

THREAD. Unless otherwise indicated, the thread is 6/0 and prewaxed. The colors mentioned are desirable but not absolutely essential. You can get by using white thread for light flies and black for dark ones.

TAIL. Feather fibers are the most common tailing material. For dry flies, they should be stiff fibers taken from good-quality rooster capes. For submerged flies, any soft feather will do in the appropriate color. More and more tiers are using hen hackle for wet tails.

BODY. Dubbed fur is the most common body medium, and the one recommended in most of these patterns. Tinsel bodies are common on streamer and bucktail flies.

WING. In tying dry flies, the wing is usually applied first. In wets, it is usually the last portion tied in. In many flies, the wing can be eliminated with little loss in effectiveness.

HACKLE. Dry flies are tied with high-quality, stiff, glossy rooster hackle. Wets are tied with hen hackle or other soft feather.

HEAD. While not specifically mentioned in most patterns, the head should be neatly wrapped following the application of the last piece of material in the recipe, a finishing knot applied, and head cement added to secure the fly. On dries, wets, and nymphs, the head is usually unobtrusive, but on streamers the head is often finished in high-gloss lacquer and eyes are painted on in some cases. A neat head is therefore critical on these flies.

Wet Flies

Blue Dun
Hook: 10–16 reg. or 2X long
    (3906)(9671)
Thread: Black
Tail: Blue dun fibers
Body: Muskrat fur
Wing: Gray duck quill sections
Hackle: Blue dun

Dark Cahill
Hook: 10–18 reg. or 2X long
    (3906) (9671)
Thread: Brown
Tail: Wood duck flank fibers
Body: Medium brown rabbit
Wing: Wood duck flank fibers
Hackle: Dark ginger

Gold-Ribbed Hare's Ear
Hook: 8–14 reg. or 2X long (3906)
    (9671)
Thread: Brown or black
Tail: Brown hackle fibers
Body: Rabbit ear fur
Ribbing: Flat gold tinsel or
    copper wire
Wing: Light gray duck quill
Hackle: Brown

Leadwing Coachman
Hook: 10–16 reg. or 2X long
    (3906) (9671)
Thread: Black
Tail: None
Body: Peacock herl
Wing: Gray duck quill
Hackle: Reddish brown

Light Cahill
Hook: 10–18 reg. or 2X long
    (3906) (9671)
Thread: Cream
Tail: Wood duck flank fibers
Body: Cream fox fur
Wing: Wood duck flank fibers
Hackle: Light ginger

March Brown
Hook: 10–14 reg. or 2X long
    (3906) (9671)
Thread: Black
Tail: Brown hackle fibers
Body: Brown rabbit fur
Ribbing: Flat gold tinsel
Wing: Dark mottled turkey quill
Hackle: Brown and grizzly, mixed

Montreal
Hook: 8–12 reg. or 2X long (3906)
    (9671)
Thread: Black
Tail: Dyed red hackle fibers
Body: Maroon floss

Ribbing: Flat gold tinsel
Wing: Dark mottled turkey quill
Hackle: Dyed maroon or red
    hackle

Parmachene Belle
Hook: 10–14 reg. or 2X long
    (3906) (9671)
Thread: Black
Tail: Red and white hackle fibers
Body: Yellow wool
Ribbing: Flat gold tinsel
Wing: White duck quill with red
    stripe
Hackle: Red and white, mixed

Royal Coachman
Hook: 10–16 reg. or 2X long
    (3906) (9671)
Thread: Black
Tail: Brown hackle fibers
Body: Peacock herl with red floss
    section in center
Wing: White duck quill
Hackle: Brown

Streamers and Bucktails

Black-Nose Dace
Hook: 2–10 4X long (79580)
Thread: Black monocord
Tail: Red yarn cut short
Body: Silver tinsel
Wing: White bucktail, black bear,
    brown bucktail, layered in
    that order
Head: Lacquered black, eyes
    optional

Muddler Minnow
Hook: 1–12 3X long (9672)
Thread: Black
Tail: Brown mottled turkey quill
Body: Flat gold tinsel

Underwing: Gray squirrel
Wing: Brown mottled turkey
    quill
Collar: Natural deer hair, flared
Head: Natural deer hair, spun
    and clipped

Marabou Muddler
Hook: 2–10 3X or 4X long (9672)
    (79580)
Thread: Black
Tail: Dyed red hackle fibers
Body: Flat silver tinsel
Wing: Marabou fibers (black,
    brown, yellow, etc.)
Head: Deer hair dyed to match
    wing, spun and clipped

Matuka Streamer
Hook: 2–10 4X long (79580) or
    up-eye salmon hook
    (36890)
Thread: Color to match fly
Tail: None
Body: Fur of choice color
Ribbing: Narrow flat tinsel, silver
    or gold
Wing: Four matched soft hackles,
    bound to hook shank with
    tinsel
Hackle: Wet fly style, color to
    match wing

Mickey Finn
Hook: 2–12 4X long (79580)
Thread: Black monocord
Tail: None

Body: Silver tinsel
Wing: Yellow bucktail, red
    bucktail, yellow bucktail,
    layered in that order
Head: Black lacquered, eyes
    optional

Shenk Sculpin
Hook: 1–8 4X long (79580)
Thread: Black
Tail: Black marabou fibers
Body: Black rabbit fur
Wing: Black marabou
Pectoral fins: Dark quill sections,
    tied in on either
    side
Head: Black deer hair, spun and
    clipped flat for
    wedge-shaped head

Dry Flies

Adams
Hook: 10–22 (94840)
Thread: Black or gray
Tail: Grizzly and brown hackle
    fibers, mixed
Body: Muskrat fur
Wings: Grizzly hackle tips
Hackle: Grizzly and brown,
    mixed

Ant
Hook: 12–22 (94840)
Thread: Black
Tail: None
Body: Black fur, wound in two
    distinct lumps
Hackle: Black, wound between
    lumps, clipped flat top
    and bottom
Note: Cinnamon ants are also
    effective

Bi-Visible
Hook: 10–22 (94840)

Tail: Hackle fibers to match fly
Body: None
Wing: None
Hackle: Color of choice tied in at
    bend and wound forward
    in tight turns creating an
    all-hackle fly. Final two
    turns with white hackle
    for visibility

Blue-Winged Olive
Hook: 16–24 (94840)
Thread: Olive
Tail: Blue dun hackle fibers
Body: Pale olive fur
Wings: Blue dun hackle tips
Hackle: Pale blue dun

Caenis (Trichorithodes)
Hook: 24, ring eye (94859)
Thread: Black or white (see
    below)
Body: Black tying thread (male) or
    white (female)

Hackle: Grizzly or blue dun
Note: Trim hackle top and bottom
for spinner pattern

Dorato Hare's Ear
Hook: 10–24 (94840)
Thread: Olive or tan
Tail: Grizzly fibers, tied half as
long as typical dry fly
Body: Hare's ear fur
Wing: Wood duck flank fibers,
undivided
Hackle: Grizzly and ginger,
mixed and trimmed flat
even with hook point

Gray Wulff
Hook: 8–12 (94840)
Thread: Black
Tail: Brown bucktail
Body: Gray wool yarn
Wing: Brown bucktail, divided
Hackle: Blue dun
Note: Wulff flies are tied in
several other colors; white,
brown, and so on.

Humpy
Hook: 8–16 (94840)
Thread: Brown
Tail: Deer hair (leave excess)
Body: Brown floss
Overbody: Tail deer hair brought
forward and tied down
Wing: White calf tail, divided
Hackle: Brown

Letort Cricket
Hook: 12–18 2X long 2X fine
(94831)
Thread: Black
Tail: None

Body: Black fur
Wing: Black duck quill, tied flat
over body
Head: Black deer hair, clipped
(leave a few strands to
suggest legs)

Letort Hopper
Hook: 8–14 2X long 2X fine
(94831)
Thread: Brown
Tail: None
Body: fur to match local hopper
(yellow is usually best)
Wing: Mottled turkey, tied flat
over body
Head: Natural deer hair, clipped
squarish like hopper head

Light Cahill
Hook: 12–22 (94840)
Thread: Cream
Tail: Pale ginger hackle fibers
Body: Cream fox fur
Wing: Wood duck flank, divided
Hackle: Pale ginger

Peacock Midge
Hook: 22–26 ring eye (94859)
Thread: White
Tail: None
Body: Peacock herl
Wing: None
Hackle: Grizzly

Royal Coachman
Hook: 8–20 (94840)
Thread: Black
Tail: Golden pheasant crest fibers
Body: Peacock herl with red floss
center
Wing: White calf tail, divided
Hackle: Dark brown

Caddis Larva
Hook: 8–16 (3906) or English bait
     style hook with
     pronounced bend (37140)
Thread: Black
Tail: None
Underbody: Green floss or yarn
Body: White latex strip wound
     over underbody in tight
     wind, creating segmented
     effect
Collar: Several turns of peacock
     herl near the head of the
     fly
Head: Black

Gold-Ribbed Hare's Ear
Hook: 8–20 2X long (9671)
Thread: Brown or olive
Tail: Wood duck flank fibers
Body: Rabbit ear fur
Ribbing: Copper wire or narrow
     gold tinsel
Wing case: Mottled dark turkey
     optional, otherwise
     swell body at thorax
Legs: Several wood duck flank
     fibers tied in on either side
     behind head

Muskrat
Hook: 8–16 reg. (3906) or 2X long
     (9671)
Thread: Gray or black
Tail: Soft grizzly fibers
Body: Muskrat underfur
Wing case: None
Legs: Two turns of soft grizzly
     hackle

Midge Nymph
Hook: 22–28 dry fly (94859)
Thread: Black or white
Tail: None
Body: Fur colored to match
     naturals
Collar: Strand of gray ostrich or
     marabou wound like
     hackle

Montana Stone
Hook: 2–10 4X long (79580)
Thread: Black
Tails: Black hackle fibers
Body: Black chenille
Thorax: Yellow chenille
Legs: Black hackle wound over
     thorax
Wing case: Black chenille
Note: The fly is often tied
     weighted

Pheasant Tail
Hook: 10–18 2X long (9671)
Thread: Brown
Tail: Three cock pheasant tail
     fibers
Body: Pheasant tail fibers,
     twisted and wrapped
Ribbing: Copper wire
Wing Case: Pheasant tail fibers
Legs: Pheasant tail fibers

Wooly Worm
Hook: 2–12 4X long (79580)
Tail: Dyed red hackle fibers
Body: Chenille in various colors
Hackle: Wound in wide turns
     from tail to head. Color to
     match chenille, or
     grizzly

B
SOURCES OF TACKLE, ACCESSORIES, AND SUPPLIES

Fly Shops

On the following pages are listed shops and stores around the country that cater to the special needs of the fly angler. Each of these shops replied to a questionnaire about their services, and those responses are noted along with the name, address, and phone number of the shops.

These shops sell fly tackle, accessories, and supplies, and they employ experienced salespeople who can aid the beginning angler in selecting equipment. In addition, most of them carry a complete line of fly-tying materials and tools, rod-building supplies, angling art and books, and outdoor clothing.

The list of shops is organized geographically to aid you in locating a shop in your immediate or nearby area. In addition to their basic services, I have listed special services provided by each establishment. These services fall into the following categories:

Casting Instruction

Casting instruction means training in basic fly casting. The instruction may be offered individually or as part of a class. Many of the shops offering casting instruction have casting facilities nearby, and a few even have stocked ponds to provide actual fishing conditions.

Fly-Tying Classes

While many of these shops offer individual help to tiers with particular problems, I have listed those that offer special classes for the beginning tier. There is often, but not always, a fee for these classes.

Rod-Building Classes

As is the case with fly tying, many shops offer advice and informal instruction to beginning rod builders. Those indicated offer regular classes.

Guide Services

Generally speaking, guide services apply to local waters only. In some cases, particularly with Rocky Mountain area shops, guide services may cover a wide area. In a few cases, world-wide angling trips are arranged.

Trial Before Purchase

This usually means that you can arrange to cast with an outfit before purchase. At some shops you must bring your own reel and line in order to try rods—check beforehand. In a very few cases the shops keep "demonstrator" outfits on hand with which you can actually fish before making up your mind.

Miscellaneous

At the end of the questionnaire card, I asked shop owners or managers to indicate any service that they offered that was unusual or that had not been described in the questionnaire. Those responses are included.

This list does not constitute a recommendation for the shops included, nor does the failure of a particular shop to appear on the list mean that such a shop does not offer all the services of those included. It has been recently estimated that more than two thousand retail businesses sell fly fishing equipment in the United States; I was able to contact only a few. Whether or not you patronize any of the shops included here, the list should give you a good idea of the kinds of services available at stores of this kind and make it easier for you to identify and to evaluate fly shops in your area.

Farrow Allen's Fly Fishing Shop
802–658–6128
200 Main Street POB 3006 /
Burlington, Vermont 05401
Casting instruction, fly-tying
classes, rod-building classes, trial
before purchase

Angler's Ruff, Ltd. 516–482–0925
576 Middle Neck Road /
Great Neck, New York 11023
Casting instruction, fly-tying
classes, rod-building, trial before
purchase. "Geared toward the
salmon angler."

Forest County Sports Center
814–755–3744
Tionesta, Pennsylvania 16353
Casting instruction, trial before
purchase

Flyfisher's Paradise 814–234–4189
Box 448, Pike Street / Lemont,
Pennsylvania 16851
Casting instruction, trial before
purchase, fly-tying aid on informal
basis

The Orvis Company, Inc.
802–302–3434
Manchester, Vermont 05254
Casting instruction, trial before
purchase, fly-fishing schools April
through August, fishing travel
service

Oliver's Orvis Shop 201–735–5959
44 Main Street, / Clifton, New
Jersey 08809
Casting instruction, guide
services, trial before purchase

The Sporting Gentleman
717–565–6140

306 E. Baltimore Avenue / Media,
Pennsylvania 19063
Casting instruction, fly-tying
classes, trial before purchase,
guide services, fly fishing classes

The Orvis Shop
5655 Main Street / Williamsville,
New York 14221
716–631–5131
1478 Marsh Road / Pittsford, New
York 14534
716–248–8390
Casting instruction, fly tying
classes, trial before purchase, rod
building components

Joe's Tackle Shop 207–448–2909
Rt. 1 Box 156 / Danforth, Maine
04424
Casting instruction, fly-tying
classes, rod-building classes,
guide services, trial before
purchase, antique rod museum

Orvis/Sporting Adventure
301–465–1112
9191 Baltimore National Pike /
Ellicott City, Maryland 21043
Casting instruction, fly-tying
classes, trial before purchase,
informal rod-building instruction

The Rivergate 914–265–2318
Rt. 9 / Cold Spring, New York
10516
Casting instruction, fly-tying
classes, guide services, trial before
purchase, catalog, coffee, and
conversation

Windsor Fly Shop 717–424–0938
348 N. 9th Street / Stroudsburg,
Pennsylvania 18360
Casting demonstrations, fly-tying

classes, trial before purchase,
stream information, extensive
book and material section

Bob Leeman's Trout Shop
207–989–4060
807 Wilson Street / Brewer,
Maine 04412
(mail) Box 1163 / Bangor, Maine
04401
Casting instruction, fly-tying
classes, guide services, trial before
purchase, Maine Atlantic Salmon
information

Angler's Pro Shop 215–362–0122
18 E. 3rd Street / Landsdale,
Pennsylvania 19466
Casting instruction, fly-tying
classes, trial before purchase,
saltwater fly tackle

Eddie's Flies and Tackle
207–945–5587
303 Broadway / Bangor, Maine
04401

Guide services, informal help with
fly tying and rod building, kits for
fly tying and rod building

The Angler 202–333–1156
1055 Thomas Jefferson Street NW
Washington, D.C. 20037
Casting instruction, fly-tying
classes, guide services,
rod-building classes, trial before
purchase, speakers provided for
fly-fishing topics, repair of all type
rods in the store

The Orvis Shop of Boston
617–653–9144
213 W. Plain Street / Wayland,
Massachusetts 01778
Casting instruction, fly-tying
classes, trial before purchase

Quiet Sports 802–247–6320
Route 7 / Brandon, Vermont
05733
Casting instruction, guide
services, trial of some outfits
before purchase

South

The Orvis Shop of Arkansas, Inc.
501–663–5121
1161 Rebsamen Park Road / Little
Rock, Arkansas 72202
Casting instruction, fly-tying
classes, guide services, trial before
purchase

Hunter Bradlee Company
214–744–1030
291 The Quadrangle 2800 Routh
Street / Dallas, Texas 75201
Casting instruction, fly-tying
classes, trial before purchase,
saltwater fly tackle

Midwest

Orvis Pole and Paddle
Brookfield, Wisconsin 53005
Casting instruction, fly-tying
classes, guide services, trial before
purchase

Anglersmail 216–884–7476
6497 Pearl Road / Cleveland, Ohio
44130
Casting instruction, fly-tying
classes, rod-building classes, trial
before purchase, catalog

Jorgensen's of Fort Wayne
219–432–5519
6226 Covington Road
Ft. Wayne, Ind. 46804
Casting instruction, trial before
purchase, fishing library, angling
trips arranged

Gates AuSable Lodge and Pro
Shop 517–348–8462
Rt. 2 Box 2336 Stephan Bridge /
Grayling, Michigan 49738
Casting instruction, fly-tying
classes, guide services, trial before
purchase

TMF Sports Shop 216–296–2614
107 E. Main Street / Ravenna,
Ohio 44266
Casting instruction, fly-tying
classes, guide services,

rod-building classes, trial before
purchase, catalog

Thornapple Orvis Shop
616–676–0177
Thornapple Village / Ada,
Michigan 49301
Casting instruction, fly-tying
classes, guide services,
rod-building classes, trial before
purchase, fly-fishing school,
entomology classes

A. J. Burrows Trout and Grouse
312–251–8090
1147 Wilmette Avenue /
Wilmette, Illinois 60091
Casting instruction, fly-tying
classes, rod-building classes, trial
before purchase, fishing
information for Wisconsin and
Michigan, entomology clinics

Rocky Mountains

Garrett's Outdoor Shop
307–367–2449
Box 909 332 W. Pine / Pinedale,
Wyoming 82941
Casting instruction, fly-tying
classes, rod-building classes,
guide services, trial before
purchase, "600 lakes and 250 miles
of float fishing"

Artful Angler 303–741–0958
7500 S. University Boulevard /
Littleton, Colorado 80122
Casting instruction, fly-tying
classes, rod-building classes,
guide services, trial before
purchase, extensive rod-building
and fly-tying equipment

The Flyfisher Ltd. 303–322–5014
315 Columbine Street / Denver,
Colorado 80206
Casting instruction, fly-tying

classes, rod-building classes,
guide services, trial before
purchase, entomology classes,
large library

Dan Bailey Flies and Tackle
406–222–1673
209 W. Park Street / Livingston,
Montana 59047
Casting instruction, guide
services, trial before purchase,
area fishing information a specialty

Wild Wings Orvis Shop
406–587–4707
2720 W. Main Street / Bozeman,
Montana 59715
Casting instruction, fly-tying
classes, rod-building classes,
guide services, trial before
purchase, extensive fly-tying and
rod-building equipment,
"excellent story-telling
department"

Angler's Retreat 208–345–3057
510 Main Street / Boise, Idaho
83702
Casting instruction, fly-tying
classes, rod-building classes,
guide services, trial before
purchase, specializing in "Idaho
System" float tubes, Stillwater
nymphs, and waders

Bud Lilly's Trout Shop
406–646–7801
West Yellowstone, Montana
59758
Casting instruction, fly-tying
classes, guide services, trial before
purchase

George Angerson's Yellowstone
Angler 406–222–7130
124 N. Main Street
Livingston, Montana 59047
Casting instruction, fly-tying
classes, rod-building classes,
guide services, demo outfits for
trial, fly fishing school, spring
creek guiding and maps

The Frustrated Fishermen
406–961–3401
Rt. 1, Box 46A / Victor, Montana
59075
Casting instruction, fly-tying

classes, rod-building classes,
guide services, trial before
purchase

Four Rivers Fishing Company
406–684–5651
205 S. Main Street / Twin Bridges,
Montana 59754
Guide services and extensive
tackle selection

Will Godfrey Fly Fishing Center
208–558–9960
PO Box 168 / Island Park, Idaho
83429
Casting instruction, guide
services, trial before purchase,
water condition and fishing
information, world-wide fishing
trips

Bob Jacklin's Fly Shop
406–646–7336
PO Box 604 / West Yellowstone,
Montana 59758
Casting instruction, guide
services, river float trips

Silver Creek Sports 208–726–5282
507 N. Main / Sun Valley, Idaho
83353
Casting instruction, fly-tying
classes, guide services, trial before
purchase, "$75,000 fly selection"

Far West

Kaufmann's Streamborn Fly Shop
503–639–7004
12963 S.W. Pacific Highway /
Portland, Oregon 97223
Casting instruction, fly-tying
classes, rod-building classes,
guide services, trial before
purchase, catalog, world-wide
angling trips

The Greased Line Fly Shoppe
206–694–9633
2700 Andresen Road / Vancouver,
Washington 98661
Casting instruction, fly-tying
classes, informal rod-building aid,
guide services, trial before
purchase

183 Hat Creek Anglers 916–335–3165
3193 Main Street / Johnson Park,
Burney, California 96013
Casting instruction, fly-tying
classes, rod-building classes,
guide services, trial before
purchase, fly fishing school,
angling photography school

Kaufmann's
Streamborn/Bellevue
206–643–2246
15015 Main Street / Bellevue,
Washington 98007
Casting instruction, fly-tying
classes, rod-building classes,
guide services, trial before
purchase, fly fishing classes, free
clinics on fly fishing topics

The Midge Fly Shop
408–263–8877
2132 O'Toole Avenue / San Jose,
California 95131
Casting instruction, fly-tying
classes, rod-building classes,
guide services, trial before
purchase, fly fishing school

The Barbless Hook 503–248–9651
23 NW 23rd Place / Portland,
Oregon 97210
Casting instruction, fly-tying
classes

Fur, Hook, and Hackle
503–772–3456
828 S. Central / Medford, Oregon
97501
Casting instruction, fly-tying
classes, rod-building classes, trial
before purchase

The Brindle Bug 503–536–2572
Aspen Valley / LaPine, Oregon
97739
Casting instruction, fly-tying
classes, guide services

The Fly Shop 916–246–9988
4140 Churn Creek Road /
Redding, California 96002
Casting instruction, fly-tying
classes, fly fishing school,
rod-building instruction, angling
information, fly fishing art gallery

Mail Order Sources

The Orvis Company
Manchester, Vermont 05254

Hackle & Tackle Company
Central Square, New York 13036

Kaufman's Streamborn Fly Shop
PO Box 23032
Portland, Oregon 97223

The Rivergate
Rt. 9, Box 275
Cold Spring, New York 10516

The Hook and Hackle Company
PO Box 1003
Plattsburgh, New York 12901

Flyfisher's Paradise
PO Box 448
Lemont, Pennsylvania 16851

Thomas & Thomas
22 Third Street
PO Box 32
Turner Falls, Massachusetts
01376

E.J. Hille: The Angler's Supply
House, Inc.
815 Railway Street,
PO Box 996
Williamsport, Pennsylvania 17701

Dan Bailey's Flies & Tackle
209 West Park St.
Livingston, Montana 59047

Bud Lilly's Trout Shop
39 Madison Ave.
West Yellowstone, Montana
59758

GLOSSARY

Attractor An angler's term for a type of fly that appears to entice fish to strike by arousing aggression, curiosity, territoriality, or some other motive other than hunger. Attractor flies are usually bright and flashy and do not closely resemble real food forms found in the stream.

Backcast A portion of a fly cast in which the line is driven above and behind the angler. When the backcast straightens in the air, the forward cast begins.

Backhand cast A cast made on the opposite side of the body from the usual, so that the backcast goes to the front of the angler and the forward cast to the rear.

Backing Small-diameter fishing line, ideally of dacron, that is attached to the core of the reel before the fly line is tied on. The backing builds up the core so that more line is taken in with each revolution of the handle. The backing also protects against a long run by a big fish.

Blood knot The most common knot used for fastening together two lengths of nylon monofilament. The blood knot cannot be used to join strands that differ in diameter by more than about 0.003.

Bodkin A handled needle that is used in tying flies. Most often the bodkin (also called the dubbing needle) is used for applying small drops of cement to finish the head of the fly.

185

Bucktails   Baitfish imitations, tied from animal hair.

Bug taper   A line designed for casting bass bugs or other large, air-resistant flies. It is a weight forward line in which much of the weight of the line is heavily concentrated in the forward portion of the taper.

Cape   A fly tier's term for the neck skin of a chicken, usually a rooster, that has been dried with the feathers still attached. Hackles are plucked from the neck and used in tying flies.

Capillary action   The process by which the fibers of material in a wet fly or nymph soak up water, causing the fly to become saturated and sink upon being cast.

Clinch knot   A simple knot for attaching the fly to tippet. In the "improved" version, a strong knot as well.

Collar   A term used to designate hackle wound on a fly, as in "a collar of dry fly hackle." The hackle in a collar is wound on edge, so that the fibers of the feather stand out at an angle from the hook shank.

Current relief   A major motive of fish in flowing water who need to find stream obstructions or other features that reduce the pressure of the current. Otherwise, the fish must constantly swim in place just to maintain its position.

Double taper   A fly line configuration in which the line gradually grows finer in diameter at each end so the portion to which the leader is attached is smaller in diameter than the middle of the line.

Drag   (1) An angler's term for the unnatural motion of a fly when it crosses the current or moves at a speed different from that of freely floating materials in the same current line. It is caused by the current pulling on the line or leader.
(2) A reel mechanism that slows the revolution of the reel spool as line is being taken off the reel. The drag prevents spool overrun and also adds resistance when a fish runs line off the reel.

Dropper   An extra stand of leader material tied in above the tippet to which an additional fly may be tied. Also, a name given to any flies so attached. Lead weight may also be attached to a dropper stand.

Dry flies   Flies designed to float on the water's surface. They represent the winged stages of aquatic insects or terrestrial insects that happen into the stream.

Dubbing   The process of spinning fur or other body material onto thread for making the bodies of fishing flies. Also, the name given to the fur or other material used in this process.

Dun   An angler's term for the first winged stage of the mayfly, known to entomologists as a subimago.

Emergence	A technical term for what fly fishermen call a "hatch." Aquatic insects develop wings and fly from the water in preparation for mating and egg-laying.
Entomology	The scientific study of insects.
False casting	Holding a fly cast in the air without allowing it to fall. False casting is most often used to flick the moisture off a dry fly, but it can also increase accuracy, since the amount of line needed to reach a given target can be measured out in false casts before the fly is allowed to drop.
Ferrule	The joint at which the sections of a rod are assembled. One portion of the ferrule (male) fits into the other (female).
Fly floatant	Material that aids in the floating of dry flies by adding water-repellent properties to the fly. Modern fly floatants are typically silicone-based and come in spray, liquid, and paste forms.
Forage fish	Food fish. Applies to any fish small enough to be regular food for larger gamefish.
Forward cast	Also called the forecast, this is the portion of the cast in which the line is cast to the front of the angler and the fly delivered to the target.
Fry	A common name for immature fish.
Guide	A rod fitting that directs the flow of the line during the cast. Guides may be of metal or ceramic material.
Hackle	Feather. It usually refers to the neck feathers of a rooster, but it may also refer to feathers from other parts of the bodies of both sexes of chickens and other birds.
Hatch	An angler's term for the emergence of aquatic insects. During the hatch, aquatic insects develop wings and fly away from the stream.
Hoods	The portions of the reel seat that fit over the feet of the reel and are then held tightly by the threaded rings.
Hook shank	The portion of the hook that lies between the eye and the bend and upon which the fly is tied.
Keeper guide	A small ring or wire guide just above the hand grip on a fly rod. It is for parking the fly when moving from one location to another.
Lateral line	A bundle of nerve fibers at the midline of a fish through which vibrations are detected. The lateral line usually appears as a dark stripe.
Leader	A section of nylon monofilament, usually tapered, which is attached to the fly line at one end and to the fly on the other.
Lies	Locations in streams where fish are known or suspected to be.

187

Line weave	A technique of retrieve in which the fly line is woven around the fingers of the line hand.
Matuka	A style of streamer fly in which the feather "wing" is bound to the hook shank at several points, usually by wrapped tinsel.
Mending line	The process of positioning the fly line on the water to avoid the tendency of the current to pull the line downstream faster than the fly, which would create drag. Most mends involve flipping a section of the line upstream.
Midge	A general term given to extremely small insects. Also, a specific name given to many small species of the Diptera family of true flies. Finally, a descriptive term for tackle to represent such tiny insects, as in "midge" fly rod.
Monofilament	Clear nylon line used in fishing. Leaders are made of monofilament.
Nymph	A name for the underwater stage of aquatic insects, or for the artificial flies that represent this stage.
Pocket	An angler's term for an area in a stream suspected of holding fish. A pocket is usually an area of reduced current stress.
Presentation	A general term for the delivery of a fly to a fish or to a location suspected of harboring a fish.
Prospecting	Fly fishing without attempting to imitate a particular insect upon which fish are known to be feeding. Generalized fly patterns like the Adams are usually used. Also known as "fishing the water."
Reel pillars	The outer frame components in a fly reel that limit the amount of line that the reel can hold.
Reel seat	A fitting below the handle on a fly rod to which the reel is fitted.
Retrieve	When used by fly anglers the term refers to any process by which the fly is brought back toward the angler's location after being cast.
Ribbing	Material wound over the body of a fly to create the impression of segmentation. It may be contrasting thread, fine wire, or tinsel.
Rise-form	The configuration of the disturbance made on the surface by a rising fish. It may indicate the insect being fed on, among other things.
Rod blank	The long piece of material (bamboo, boron, glass, graphite) that forms the basis of the rod. The handle, guides, and other fittings are attached to make the completed rod.
Roll cast	A cast in which the line is drawn toward the angler on the surface and rolled out again with a forward stroke of the rod.

Running line	Small-diameter line that shoots through the rod guides easily, and allows greater distance in casting.
Shooting line	Synonymous with running line.
Sink rate	A measure of the speed with which a sinking line sinks. Different conditions call for lines of differing sink rates.
Sink-tip	A fly line in which the forward portion of the line sinks while the remainder floats. In most sink-tip lines, the sinking portion is ten feet long. Lines with longer sinking portions are called "sink-heads," or "sink-tapers," or "sink-bellies."
Slip strike	A strike technique in which the line is deliberately allowed to slip or slide through the fingers. It is used with delicate leader tippets where a typical strike technique would snap the tippet.
Snake cast	Also known as the "S-cast," "wiggle cast," and so on, the snake cast is used to prolong the drag-free drift of the fly. It is made by waving the rod from side to side upon completion of the power stroke so the line falls to the surface in a series of curves.
Snake guide	The fine wire guides on a typical fly rod.
Spawning	Refers to the reproductive activities of fish. Technically, it refers to the act of egg fertilization, but it is commonly used to designate the whole reproductive process, which includes migration, nest preparation, courtship behavior, and so on.
Spinner	The sexually mature stage of the mayfly life cycle, called the imago by entomologists.
Splat cast	A cast in which the fly is splashed down hard on the water to represent the landing of a terrestrial insect.
Split-cane	Refers to the construction of bamboo fly rods, which are made from strips of bamboo split from the original plant and glued together.
Spook	A jargon term used by anglers meaning "to frighten."
Streamers	Baitfish imitations, tied from feathers.
Stretcher	The end fly in a multi-fly cast.
Stripping guide	The first guide from the handle on a fly rod. It is a ring guide in most cases.
Stripping line	A method of retrieving line in which the fly is manipulated in a series of jerks or pulls.
Surgeon's knot	A simple knot for joining two strands of monofilament. It has the advantage of working well with two strands of quite different diameters.

189

Taper	In fly lines, a gradual change in diameter at some point or points in the line. In leaders, a gradual reduction in diameter from the butt, which is attached to the fly line, to the tippet, onto which the fly is tied.
Terrestrial	A land insect. They sometimes happen into the water and become fish food. Ants and grasshoppers are examples.
Tippet	The last and smallest portion of a fly leader, onto which the fly is attached.
Tip-top	The top guide on a fly rod.
Tube knot	A knot named for the tube that is used in constructing it. Commonly used to attach leader to fly line.
Turle knot	A knot for attaching the fly to the tippet in which the knot is tied on the head of the fly. Although not particularly strong, the turle knot provides exact alignment between the hook and the tippet.
Wet flies	Flies designed to be fished under water. They are tied of absorbent materials and may represent underwater food forms.
Window	A term describing the small area through which the fish can look through the surface and see objects above the water.

INDEX